I0414461

AN ALMOST FATAL MIRACLE

AN ALMOST FATAL MIRACLE

✦

REALIZING REALITY

Roger Daniel Rizzo

iUniverse, Inc.
New York Lincoln Shanghai

AN ALMOST FATAL MIRACLE
REALIZING REALITY

Copyright © 2008 by Roger Daniel Rizzo

All rights reserved. No part of this book may be used or reproduced by any means, graphic, electronic, or mechanical, including photocopying, recording, taping or by any information storage retrieval system without the written permission of the publisher except in the case of brief quotations embodied in critical articles and reviews.

iUniverse books may be ordered through booksellers or by contacting:

iUniverse
2021 Pine Lake Road, Suite 100
Lincoln, NE 68512
www.iuniverse.com
1-800-Authors (1-800-288-4677)

Because of the dynamic nature of the Internet, any Web addresses
or links contained in this book may have changed
since publication and may no longer be valid.

The views expressed in this work are solely those of the author and do not necessarily reflect the views of the publisher, and the publisher hereby disclaims any responsibility for them.

ISBN: 978-0-595-43962-1 (pbk)
ISBN: 978-0-595-68980-4 (cloth)
ISBN: 978-0-595-88282-3 (ebk)

Printed in the United States of America

Contents

Introduction

My life changed drastically in one day. On June 30, 1995, I was in a horrible motorcycle accident just north of San Francisco. Unfortunately, I was not wearing a helmet or any protective clothing at the time.

The accident left my body battered and crushed; head trauma left me in danger of becoming a vegetable. I was hospitalized for over six months, and many doctors told me that I would die. But despite my horrendous injuries, I survived. Nevertheless, every aspect of my life was immensely altered by the accident. With no warning whatsoever, everything changed: my social status, my home, my family, my job, my friendships, and my dreams. And yet it is my carefully considered opinion that my life has vastly improved since my horrible accident, despite the overwhelming tragedy I experienced. This book explains why and describes how my entire way of thinking concerning life has significantly changed.

In substance, I miraculously overcame seemingly fatal medical injuries and the antagonism of people around me. Since then, my relationships with God, Jesus, and the Holy Spirit have become much stronger and largely occupy my thoughts. I believe that my increased contact with these divinities has also resulted in the development of my own personal recognition of the meaning and purpose of life.

My primary goal now is to assist people who are poor, elderly, or ill, either physically or mentally. I would like to help them appreciate what existence on Earth is truly about so they will not be overly depressed by their conditions. In part, that is why I wrote this book.

My primary purpose in preparing this book, however, is to benefit the lives of many others. I passionately want to help people relinquish their obsession with what I now believe are meaningless goals and desires.

1

My Life before the Tragic Accident

Before the accident, my priority system was seriously flawed. While ambition is ordinarily admirable, mine was out of control. My thirst for success left me restless, unable to stop pushing myself. I was not just ambitious, I was obsessed. My drive led me to great success, measured by ordinary social standards. However, I failed to focus on what I now believe really matters in life. Ironically, my obsessive tendency endured beyond my accident and enabled me to miraculously recover from my near-fatal injuries. And since the accident, this tendency has also allowed me to focus almost exclusively on what I have concluded truly matters in life.

To enable the reader to gauge the impact the accident had on my life, it is necessary to describe in some detail the type of individual I was before that fortuitous day. The reader will then be able to compare what I believed was of critical significance before and after the time I spent on death's doorstep.

My Education

Even as I was growing up and maturing, I was very much motivated to achieve. Consistent with my propensity to achieve, I decided to attend college and obtain three different degrees.

I began attending California State University, Chico, in 1972. During my initial year of college, one class really stands out in my memory: ballroom dancing. I learned how to do the jitterbug, the fox-trot, the waltz, the rumba, the samba, and so on. I think the reason it is especially memorable for me is that back then, I was extremely well coordinated, but since my accident, I have been completely uncoordinated, to say the least.

Between my second and third years of college, I and several friends decided to move to Torrance, California. A few days after registering for college at California State University, Dominguez Hills, I found a job delivering water softener tanks and bags of salt to Culligan customers throughout southern California.

This Culligan job was memorable for me for unusual reasons. The water softener tanks and bags of salt ordinarily had to be placed in the customers' backyards, which were often fenced to keep their dogs from escaping. That meant the dogs often confronted me for invading their territory. I still vividly remember a delivery in Hermosa Beach, California. I went into a fenced backyard where a huge dog was feasting on its breakfast on an elevated back porch. I had to deliver two bags of salt to the water softening machine. The dog didn't even look up at me when I crossed in front of him to deliver the first bag. It wasn't until after I delivered the second bag and was half way back across the patio that the dog looked up from where it had finished its breakfast and began snarling at me. It was immediately obvious that I wouldn't reach the back gate before the huge dog had sunk its teeth deeply into my head, neck, or back. I quickly decided I had to strike the first blow. So, as the dog leaped up from the back porch to bite me, I moved toward it and kicked out in front of me with one of my boots. Much to my relief, my boot struck first, and the dog yelped and returned to the back porch with a paw over its nose.

The time I spent in Torrance was exhilarating. I learned a great deal at college and earned excellent grades. Despite getting attacked by dogs once or twice a week for over a year, I really had many adventures and a great deal of fun delivering for Culligan. I also explored nearly the entire area from Santa Barbara down to San Diego.

I returned to Chico after a little more than a year and again became a student at California State University, Chico, for my senior year of college. To finance my schooling, I also worked several days a week.

I decided at that point in my education to major in international relations, with a special focus on the Soviet Union, which was then still the primary communist nation in the world. I graduated with distinction in 1976. I had a degree in international relations, but no concrete plans for what to do with it. I have never been employed in the area in which I obtained my undergraduate degree. The primary use of my college studies was when I traveled abroad and assessed the people living in the places that had been the subject of my studies.

Nevertheless, I have no regrets about living in Chico and attending college there. My undergraduate course of study was fascinating. Moreover, I made many wonderful friendships in Chico that I plan to maintain for the rest of my life. Last, Chico was a wonderful place to live; it is an extremely picturesque small city and has one of the largest city parks in the United States running through the center of the town.

After obtaining my undergraduate degree, I enrolled in the master's degree program at San Francisco State University. My specific area of study was business administration with a specialty in finance. This was a full-time, two-year program. Once again, to be able to afford my education, I worked several days a week while also attending classes. I found the business classes different from the courses I had attended in Chico. I also found life in the large city of San Francisco distinctly different from life in the small college town of Chico. I quickly became engrossed in the business and finance courses. I enjoyed the subjects taught in those classes and labored to such a degree that I received singular academic honors.

Shortly after I obtained my MBA in 1979, I enrolled at University of California's Hastings College of the Law in San Francisco. The legal profession captivated me because I was amazed by a career in which I could play such an integral role in other people's economic, social, and even ethical lives. Furthermore, people requested that I play this role and paid me to legally represent them.

During my three years of law school, I continued to work almost full time. I also lived in an apartment near the ocean in San Francisco. Once again, I was so busy with education and work that I spent almost all of my time thinking about ordinary sorts of human achievements. I served on a special legal scholastic committee at Hastings. I studied legal subjects almost tirelessly. My educational efforts resulted in my being awarded a Juris Doctor from Hastings in 1982.

Through my education, I gained substantial knowledge in my fields of study and obtained the credentials I would need to find employment in several areas, all of which were highly paid. Nevertheless, I devoted very little time and effort to determining the *meaning and purpose* of my existence here on Earth.

My Employment

Like most teenagers in the United States, I held a variety of commonplace jobs. But in the summer of my junior year in high school, I did something unusual for individuals of my age. I went to Phoenix, Arizona, several hundred miles from my home in Chico to work as an apprentice electrician. I felt as though this was the first job I held that was intellectually challenging. I completely enjoyed the three months I spent installing electrical systems in homes in the Phoenix area. When I returned to Chico after that summer, I found part-time work as an electrician during my senior year of high school. In addition to electrical work on homes, I also began installing electrical wiring in apartment complexes and in a few commercial buildings. Again, I felt as though I was performing professional duties.

After enrolling at California State University, Chico, I continued to do electrical work, working part time during the academic year and full time during the summers. My electrical knowledge and skills substantially expanded during this time. When I relocated to San Francisco in 1977 to obtain my MBA, I again continued doing electrical work. Several months after completing the MBA program, I had gained sufficient experience and decided to take the California State Electrical Contractor's License examination. I passed the exam and was awarded my electrical contractor's license in October of 1979.

From 1979 until I completed my second year of law school in 1981, I did part-time electrical work, largely for another electrical contractor. I worked in homes, apartment complexes, and businesses all over the city of San Francisco. It was invigorating, concrete work, which was very different from the theoretical work of legal study.

During my second summer of law school, I was offered a position as a summer clerk with a medium-sized San Francisco law firm. My three months working there were unremarkable in that my main duties involved doing legal research and preparing motion papers and briefs for legal partners and associates. I didn't meet or interact with any clients. Nor was I able to assess how my efforts were going to make a difference in anyone's life.

Before graduating from Hastings, I did obtain an employment offer from Sedgwick, Detert, Moran, and Arnold. This firm was composed only of attorneys who actually tried civil cases. I accepted that firm's offer because I had no doubt that I wanted to be a trial attorney. The status of being a successful trial attorney and the enticing remuneration were things I could not resist. It was also definitely my desire to have a direct effect on people's lives, at least the kind of effect that results from successful legal cases. I was employed by the Sedgwick Law Offices for approximately thirteen years. The firm grew substantially during my tenure there. In 1995, it had offices in San Francisco, Los Angeles, Chicago, New York, London, and Zurich, employing approximately five hundred attorneys.

During the time that I worked as a civil trial attorney, I felt I was finally living my dream. I tried approximately thirty cases. I won all of them. I believe I succeeded because I was always honest and forthcoming with my clients, the judges, and the juries involved. Several of these cases were reputed to be among the largest in the United States and took several months to try in the various venues.

When I had a break in my busy trial schedule, which was infrequent, I very much enjoyed an activity that was different from my employment: scuba diving. I recall on one occasion, my brother and I, along with a mutual friend, drove up the California coastline to the northern part of the state. We arrived at a beach where the waves were huge and scores of large logs were being tossed around in the ocean. Since the three of us had driven so far, we decided to put on our scuba gear and go diving right away, even though the surface of the water appeared treacherous. We entered the water together but were immediately split up by the churning waves and strong current. I quickly decided to go underwater to avoid the gigantic waves. I was under the water for just seconds before the current smashed me into some rocks. My regulator came out of my mouth, and I had to surface immediately to breathe once again. I knew that at all costs, I had to survive the immense waves, avoid the logs, and make it back to shore. After what seemed like a long time, I made it to shore and located my brother. He also appeared dazed and shocked. Our friend, however, had not made it back, but he was later pulled out of the ocean by a police helicopter.

After this adventure it became clear to me that my primary hobby was similar to my career in one important respect: they both involved substantial risks. The risks were distinctly different, but they both involved possibly life-altering events for me and others. Despite the substantial risks, my career involved a great number of successes, at least when seen from the standpoint of what many regard as significant human achievements. And I did assist individuals in a variety of ways and received generous compensation. Nevertheless, my focus was not on the activities that I now believe *truly matter in life*.

My Travels

Ever since I was a young adult, I have been enamored with traveling. I have been interested in examining other individuals' lifestyles, especially in countries other than the United States. I was never certain why it was so captivating, but I think it was because the diversity of norms, ethics, and religious beliefs always fascinated me.

I began my traveling adventures during my first year of college at California State University, Chico. At the beginning of my second semester in 1973, I decided to drop out of college temporarily. I traveled to Oahu, Hawaii, and got an apartment in Waikiki, a few hundred yards from the beach.

I went to Oahu with my best friend and his girlfriend, who was also a close acquaintance of mine. By the time the three of us arrived on the island, the transportation expenses had absorbed most of our resources, leaving us with only a few dollars to pay for lodging and food. We were acutely aware of our monetary dilemma, so all three of us immediately began searching for employment. Fortunately, all three of us prevailed in our efforts. I obtained employment as a dishwasher in a restaurant that catered principally to tourists. My two friends also immediately obtained employment in service-related jobs.

My best friend met an Australian sailor who told us that he was on an extended leave from the Australian Navy. And then my friend's girlfriend met a woman who was a prostitute but told us she wanted to obtain a legitimate job and pursue a real career. The sailor and the prostitute both requested that we permit them to stay several days in our apartment. In an effort to help them, we agreed. However, our attempt to assist both of them clearly failed. A few weeks after the Australian sailor began residing with us, officers from the United States Border Patrol entered our apartment and arrested him. As they were escorting him away, they confided to us that he had left his ship without permission and had eluded the Australian military for quite some time. The woman did manage to obtain employment as a waitress during the day, but at night she often left the apartment to engage in her old career with tourists. After a few weeks, she could not resist the lure of the money and all the male attention, so she returned to her former employment and moved out of the apartment.

I remained on Oahu for a few months. When I wasn't working, I spent much of my time swimming and diving in the ocean. I also took many trips throughout parts of the island and became reasonably familiar with its history and geography.

After returning to the mainland, I saved enough money to travel to Europe. And that is precisely what I did next.

I took a bus from California to Vancouver, Canada. From Canada, I flew to London, England. When I got off the plane in the London airport, it dawned on me, and I still remember it to this day, that I was alone; I knew no one and knew no places in London to stay or even visit. Even though I was only eighteen, I quickly overcame my negative thoughts. I viewed traveling in Europe as a challenge and was determined to overcome every obstacle. I began staying at youth hostels. I also visited scores of tourist sights in downtown London, including the Parliament, the Tower of London, the London Bridge, and an almost limitless number of museums, churches, and historic sites.

What surprised me was that soon after I arrived in England, I made many friends. I met numerous people from various parts of the world who were traveling throughout England to gain some insight into the historic role England has played in the world's development. Several of these people became my friends. I also became acquainted with some local British residents who were gracious to me.

After London, I visited southern England. The aspect of the country that was most memorable was that the people there, just as in most parts of the United States that I had seen, were to a large extent fixated on their economic existence. They focused on their jobs, their homes, and what they could afford to purchase with cash or on credit.

From England, I traveled to France. Initially I went to Paris. Like London, Paris is rich with historic landmarks. Paris also abounds with some of the world's most treasured artworks. I had never been really drawn to art up to that point in my life. Nevertheless, I remember seeing in the Louvre in Paris a myriad of paintings that seemed to cry out a message to me.

I stayed in a youth hostel on the outskirts of Paris and met many others who were traveling throughout Europe. Together, we took a tour on the Seine River, went to the Eiffel Tower, visited the Champs Elysees (one of the most famous streets in the world), explored the Arc de Triomphe, and viewed many of the museums, churches, and historic sites.

After several days in the city, I went sightseeing around the French countryside and visited many castles. I finally traveled to the French Riviera. It was my impression that despite the differences in language and culture, the French were very much like the British in their preoccupation with their economic condition.

I continued south until I entered Spain. I went to Barcelona, along the Mediterranean coast to Valencia, and over to Madrid. I then visited the southern portion of Spain down to the Strait of Gibraltar. I found the Spanish people to be usually friendly and helpful. Like the European countries I visited earlier, Spain was filled with historical monuments. In one of the ports along the Mediterranean that I visited, I saw life-size replicas of the *Niña*, the *Pinta*, and the *Santa Maria*.

I crossed the Strait of Gibraltar and entered Morocco. I traveled through Morocco, Algeria, and Tunisia. These countries were materially different from the United States and the European countries I had visited thus far. The political systems, economies, and social structures were all unlike those of Western nations. Perhaps the most striking difference was the religion. These nations were Islamic. In college, I had studied the followers of Islam, but what I learned from my textbooks was very different from what I was witnessing on a personal level; here there were entire cultures following the teachings of the Prophet Muhammad. My interactions with the people of those countries were captivating, though it was extremely difficult for me to communicate with most residents in these Arab countries because of language barriers. At various times during the day, I witnessed large groups of people bowing down in the streets and giving praise to Allah. I recall thinking how remarkable it was to publicly observe large segments of the population periodically giving such praise.

After a brief time, I returned to Europe and went to Italy. Initially, I stayed in Rome. Rome abounds with relics from two and even three thousand years ago. The Italians have preserved many relics from the days when the ancient Romans controlled much of the world. I recall walking one afternoon through the remnants of the ancient Coliseum. Even more stimulating for me, though, was viewing St. Peter's Cathedral, the Vatican, the Sistine Chapel, and other historic landmarks of Roman Catholicism. The symbolic significance of these places felt overwhelming, although at the time I was not sure why. I continued my sightseeing tour in Florence, Venice, and northern Italy. Once again, these places were inspiring for their beauty, shown in their artwork and their rivers, canals, and landscapes.

From Italy I went to Switzerland, Austria, what was then Yugoslavia, Albania, and finally into Greece. I spent several days in each country and explored the mountains, cities, and ancient artifacts. Based upon my observations, I determined that each nation, although close to the others, had developed its own culture and political system. In fact, in 1974, Yugoslavia was a thriving communist country closely aligned with the Soviet Union.

I remained in Greece for many weeks and carefully explored its important connection to the distant past. I visited the Acropolis and all the historical Greek museums and institutions in the major cities, especially Athens. I personally determined that Greek and

Italian cultures were now completely different from the days when those nations were supreme world powers. It reminded me that cultural dominance is a cyclical phenomenon; nations may rule for a segment of mankind's history, but it is indisputable that rulers will change with the passage of time.

Like Greece and Italy, which controlled the world for long periods, I, too, was at the peak of my social influence before my accident, especially given my successes as a civil trial attorney. My accident caused me to realize, however, that periods of social dominance end for humans as well.

In Athens I rented an automobile and drove back through Yugoslavia and into Hungary, Poland, and Germany. Again, I was completely fascinated by the people and cultures I encountered.

I traveled on to Denmark, to a farm immediately south of Copenhagen. One of my traveling companions in Greece had relatives who owned the farm. They were very hospitable to me. They even offered me a short-term job on the farm caring for livestock. I felt, though, that I needed to resume college, so I respectfully declined. Then I traveled south again through Germany and entered the Netherlands. After briefly exploring the sights, I flew back to California from Amsterdam.

I did not travel overseas again until 1976, after I graduated from California State University, Chico. I spent many months on this next trip, circumnavigating the globe and visiting many countries. Initially, I flew to London from San Francisco and spent time again traveling through England and the countries I had visited before in Western Europe.

Then I flew from Athens, Greece, to Israel. For me, Israel was an enthralling country. It was a country imbued with both the old and new. In the old parts of cities, I explored a great deal and witnessed how little livelihoods and accommodations had changed in many centuries. The newer parts of cities seemed to me to be very much like the United States. I was particularly impressed by Jerusalem. I traveled on the same path that Jesus did over two thousand years ago when he was crucified. Israel was full of memorable places and objects relating back to history-changing events. At the time I was not sure why, but I felt extremely moved by the experiences.

I took a ship from Tel Aviv, Israel, to Istanbul, Turkey. Istanbul is a large city and has many artifacts dating to the time when it was the nexus between Europe and Asia. Though I was in Turkey for only a brief time, it seemed to me that the country was largely a combination of European and Asian influences. Everywhere I turned I witnessed how poor the vast majority of the people were in Turkey. Many of the local residents whom I met appeared to be struggling to avoid destitution.

In Istanbul I met a bus driver who was transporting approximately thirty-five young travelers from around the world all the way across southern Asia to India. At night the travelers stayed at youth hostels or slept along the side of the road in sleeping bags. After the bus driver assured me that he would make it all the way to India, I signed on and became the next passenger. During the trip across southern Asia, the bus traveled throughout each country and the travelers were able to see all the major historic points and places of interest. The bus was old and the trip took a few months to complete.

It was always interesting for me in that I was able to directly observe the interactions between the young travelers, who were often set in the ways of the places they hailed from, and local inhabitants, who practiced their own local customs and strict beliefs. There seemed to be controversy on an almost endless number of issues.

From Turkey, the bus went into Syria, Iraq, and Iran. I clearly recall that those counties were also very poor and the religion everywhere in those nations was Islam. I had a definite intuition that the Islamic people had an outlook about life that was very different from individuals in Western cultures.

In Kabul, Afghanistan, I became seriously ill and got off the bus. Among other symptoms, I had an exceedingly high fever and was extremely weak. I also could not eat any food or drink any fluids. I was unable to find doctors or medical treatment facilities that I could use in Kabul. Therefore, even though I was extremely ill, I took local transportation to Islamabad, Pakistan. Unfortunately, I was unable to locate any medical assistance in Islamabad either. For several days I simply remained in the room I had rented in a dilapidated motel and laid in bed. I was intensely feverish at times and ate nothing. But because I was obsessed with succeeding in all endeavors, I prevailed over even this extreme bout of fever. My condition wondrously improved over the next few days, and I eventually boarded a Pakistani bus and headed into India.

Once in India, I journeyed directly to New Delhi. I went to a youth hostel there. To my shock and amazement, I saw my former bus driver in the lobby. He had arrived in New Delhi alone, with none of the passengers who had been with me on the bus. Travelers had left the bus periodically as we were moving across southern Asia and encountered some treacherous situations, but there were at least twenty who made it to Afghanistan with me. I frankly asked the bus driver what happened to all those passengers. He told me that after I left the bus in Kabul, it continued up to northern Afghanistan to tour all the historic and scenic sites. While the passengers were out visiting a small village, a radical Muslim confronted the passengers and took out a pistol and shot and killed one of the young English female travelers. The other passengers were so shocked that the local authorities simply let the murderer go free that they all decided to return to Europe immediately.

At that juncture, I deeply sympathized with the other passengers and understood their concerns that their lives were much more in peril because of their travels in Asia. It is ironic that my ultimate decision at that time to continue on with my travels was the same as it would be today, but for completely different reasons. Back then I thought I had already completed my travels in the primarily Islamic countries where there may have been more Muslim terrorists. Today, I believe life here on Earth is so transitory that the value of personally witnessing entirely different cultures, remarkably different lifestyles, and fundamentally different worship systems for the Almighty far exceeds the possibility that my life here on Earth may unexpectedly be shortened.

I remained in India for approximately two months. It was an intensely populated country stricken with immense poverty. I recall walking around New Delhi and thinking that this was the most striking place I had ever been to because of the scarcity of resources for its overwhelming population. I traveled down to central India and visited many towns along the Ganges River and many remote Indian cities and villages away from the river. I also spent the good part of a day walking through the Taj Mahal, which from my experience, was singular in its construction. Then I traveled on Indian buses with scores of locals up to northern India and into Kashmir. Srinagar is the principle town in Kashmir, and many of its locals live in dilapidated houseboats on Dal Lake. I also lived in one of those houseboats for a few days.

Kashmir is located in the Himalayas. While I was in Srinagar, it came to my attention that two Hindu holy men were going to ride donkeys to a venerated cave up in the mountains and remain there briefly to give praises to their deities. They asked me if I wanted to join them. I immediately accepted their invitation. We took a bus to an eastern site in Kashmir. There we mounted three donkeys. We rode the donkeys for quite some time until we reached a height of eighteen thousand feet, where the cave was located in the mountainside. We had been traveling through snow and ice almost continuously since we mounted the donkeys. It never dawned on me to withdraw from the journey, as I was again obsessed with succeeding in my endeavors. The cave appeared to be hewn out of a steep cliff face. It went back into the hard rock about thirty feet. We remained in the cave for two days, and the Hindu holy men almost continuously praised their divine beings.

Next, I flew in an old Indian plane over the Himalayas from Srinagar to Calcutta. Of all the Indian places I visited, I was most shocked by Calcutta. It was exceedingly overpopulated I thought, even for India. The people there all seemed exceptionally poor. I distinctly remember seeing people in the streets of Calcutta dying from starvation and the sweltering heat. The most notable person I met during my travels was Mother Teresa. She had a motel in Calcutta where I stayed for a few days. She and I met and had brief discussions about the impoverished conditions in Calcutta.

From Calcutta I took local transportation through Bangladesh, Burma, and into Thailand. The food and marketplaces of Thailand really stand out in my mind. I thought Thai food was delicious. I also thought that many Thai marketplaces were completely different from any I had been to in the United States, because the people and animals, which were very diverse, were not in stores or buildings, instead they were in fields, alongside roads, or on boats in lakes and rivers.

I was now entering parts of Asia where religion was distinctly different from countries of the Middle East and India. No longer were there any mosques or Hindu centers of worship. Now the main religious centers were Buddhist temples and monasteries. The philosophies of the indigenous cultures were also noticeably different. I had never been in a Buddhist temple before and had never met or conversed with a Buddhist about their religion. What appeared really strange to me then was that Buddhists did not believe in God or any divine entity. They seemed to meditate almost incessantly and believed in attaining nirvana, or personal fulfillment. I attended Catholic schools and for many years almost never missed a Catholic mass, so it was not clear to me why people followed the Buddhist faith.

I remained in Thailand for many days and then flew to Hong Kong and very briefly visited mainland China. From there I went to Taiwan, South Korea, and Japan. My trip was drawing to an end, so my stay in each of these places was short. But I do recall visiting major historic sites in each country and getting some sense of the population's values and religious beliefs. It was fascinating for me at the time, as I was still a young and relatively inexperienced man from the United States.

I flew from Tokyo back to California. I remained in San Francisco for two years, completing all the coursework in the MBA program at San Francisco State University. After I obtained my MBA in 1979, I began my next trip, which involved circumnavigating the globe from the opposite direction. Rather than describing this trip in detail, let me just say it took many months and involved traveling through the Soviet Union and northern Europe.

I hope that at this point the reader of this memoir has a clearer understanding of the type of individual I was before my accident. I had a thirst for success, and it was only natural that I felt compelled to travel around the world as much as was sensible, given my youth and standing in life. I also felt that I would never regret having a personal understanding of the major economic, political, social, and religious systems of the world.

My Relationship with God

My parents were both staunch Roman Catholics. Therefore, I was born and baptized a Catholic. I attended St. Gregory's elementary school. As was expected, I went to mass every Sunday and observed all the holy days. I also went to confession regularly. I was an altar boy during grade school. As I became a young adult, I also served as a lector at masses. In my adult years, even though I was busy pursuing my education and my employment, I continued to attend mass weekly and serve as lector. I also did this whenever possible when I was traveling overseas.

Back before my near-fatal accident, I did not question anything taught by the Catholic Church. I simply accepted the statements about God, Jesus Christ, and the Holy Spirit without even thinking about what such statements actually meant for me. I was leading the type of life in which I was satisfied that I would sufficiently meet God's requirements as long as I attended mass every Sunday, did not blatantly commit sins, and treated others in a fair, honest way. Moreover, I was far too busy in my work and with family responsibilities to devote any real time to considering what God really wanted me to accomplish during my brief life here on Earth.

Then on June 30, 1995, my entire existence on Earth changed. I was on the very doorsteps of death for many months. I was in a coma for six weeks. I have no memory whatsoever, even to this day, of the first five and a half months I was hospitalized. Of course, my spiritual life was just like every other important aspect of my life before that almost fatal but miraculous accident. The man you have just read about in the preceding pages essentially disappeared on June 30, 1995, leaving the current individual who authored this book in his place. June 30, 1995, marks the true beginning of this story and the true beginning of my life in reality.

2

June 30, 1995

June 30, 1995, was a life-transforming day for me. The day began normally, but that is exactly the opposite of the way the day ended.

It was a routine Thursday morning. I went to work at the Sedgwick law firm as usual. I was in the toxic tort department in my law firm. Both I and the other attorneys in that department were ordinarily assigned to handle all the incoming toxic tort cases referred to our law office in San Francisco. Additionally, the attorneys in my department were also assigned to many cases outside the auspices of the department if the cases involved some form of civil litigation. I don't remember at all what transpired that day, but other attorneys in my law firm say that the most notable tasks I performed that morning were preparing legal discovery papers and orally arguing a motion at the San Francisco courthouse.

All the attorneys in the department left in the afternoon on June 30, 1995, and proceeded to a restaurant in Tiburon. Tiburon is a medium-size town approximately fifteen miles due north of San Francisco. A dinner party was being held at the restaurant to celebrate a large trial victory. There were approximately fifty people attending the event. All the trial lawyers from the department were there, as well as their spouses and division paralegals and clerks.

The party soon degenerated into a competitive festival among the trial attorneys, including me. We began boasting about trials in which we caught witnesses who'd given false testimony on the stand when we questioned them during cross-examination. As the evening continued, more alcoholic beverages were consumed, and many of the trial attorneys began conveying to our entire group what were the biggest, most monetarily perilous, or longest cases they had ever tried. This type of entertainment continued for several hours. Just as attorneys can typically be when they are so motivated, we were loud and took control of much of the restaurant. The consumption of beer and wine did not make us any less outgoing. There was a torrent of laughter and jokes the entire evening.

At restaurant closing time, an associate in my law office offered to give me a ride home on the back of his motorcycle. At that time, I was a high-level partner in the law firm. I accepted the associate's offer for transportation, as I didn't want to have to locate a bus or taxi to take me home that evening. I had no idea at the time, but as a result of that decision, my life would be radically transformed. As a result of that decision, my career, my family life, my friendships, and my hopes and dreams would be drastically altered. As a result of that decision, my entire thought process about the meaning and purpose of life here on Earth would be forever changed.

Neither the associate, who owned the motorcycle, nor I remember what happened after we left the celebration. Based on police records and ambulance reports, the following events occurred. The associate and I did not bother to wear helmets when we began our motorcycle ride that evening. In fact, we were not wearing any protective clothing at all. We headed for a drive along a road in Tiburon overlooking the San Francisco Bay. At some point, our motorcycle left the road and careened down the hill toward the bay. No other vehicle was involved in the incident. The associate and I were both thrown off the motorcycle. Our bodies were catapulted down the hillside and smashed against a score of rocks and boulders landscaping the side of the hill immediately overlooking the bay. I have absolutely no recollection of what caused the motorcycle to leave the road. Neither does my associate. We were both drinking alcohol at the party that evening, so neither of us remembers any specifics. The accident may have been caused by excessive drinking or it may not have. Nobody to this day actually knows the answer to that question.

My bruised, battered, and bloodied body finally slid to a stop approximately twelve feet above the water of the San Francisco Bay. I was airlifted by helicopter and rushed to John Muir Trauma Center in Walnut Creek, many miles to the east of the accident site. My medical records confirm that as a result of the accident I suffered severe brain injury, broken bones, overstretched and torn tendons and ligaments, and bruised muscles in my face, chest, back, hips, and legs. There were massive contusions all over my body. I could no longer breathe, so I had to have a tube inserted through my nose into my esophagus. Immediate surgery was performed on my skull to insert a shunt that would relieve the continuous bleeding. Through surgical means, a tube was inserted through my body into my heart to maintain its continuous, proper operation. I couldn't see, smell, hear, or feel because of the myriad injuries over my entire body.

I survived. I hovered near death in a deep coma for about forty days. According to my family members, I gradually came out of the comatose state. On each successive day I regained a little more brain activity. When I became semiconscious again, I was moved by ambulance to Kentfield Rehabilitation Hospital in Marin County.

At times I would sit upright in a wheelchair, tied in of course, staring into space endlessly. I did not recognize anyone or anything and ordinarily did not make any voluntary movements. I was unable to eat food for several months, so a tube had been inserted through my mouth, down my throat, and into my stomach to feed me. After being fed through a tube for approximately four months, the muscles in my mouth and jaw atrophied. The muscle tone has still not completely returned. It is sometimes difficult even now for me to eat. My right vocal cord is also permanently paralyzed. This has largely impaired my speaking ability. It also makes me cough a good deal, and I often have to clear my throat.

Because of the plethora of physical and mental problems caused by my severe brain injury, I largely forgot what transpired in my life during the five years before the accident. I also could not remember pivotal facts in several of my personal relationships. Even a basic understanding of elementary aspects of existence like eating food, drinking fluids, speaking, cleansing, and ordinary thinking eluded me. I had to slowly relearn nearly everything.

3

Hospital and Rehabilitation Center Experience

I was hospitalized for approximately six months following my accident. I look upon it as positive that because of my severe, traumatic brain injury, I was not cognizant of and do not at all remember the first five and a half months of my hospital experience. My family tells me that during this time I was a pitiful sight. Massive medical treatments were administered around the clock. The medical practitioners had inserted multiple devices into many different parts of my body. Machines did all the breathing for me and kept my blood flowing. Another machine fed me nutrients and liquids. Another machine cleansed me. Another machine removed my excrement. It is a vast understatement to say that I was a sight to behold. Throughout the hospitalization, my head was kept shaved to enable the medical practitioners to treat me.

At Kentfield I was placed on an upright board for a long period of time to stimulate my blood pressure to return to normal. Then I was placed on a bed, but my arms and legs were strapped to metal restraints to prevent me from injuring myself. Next, I was fitted with metal shoes to keep me from falling backward. When I had finally recovered sufficiently to use a wheelchair, I had to be bound into the device. A seemingly long time followed that advance. I slowly learned how to use the bathroom again, to communicate by making drawings on a tablet, and to attempt to improve my balance while lying down or sitting.

Many of the doctors told my family early on during my medical care that I was most probably going to die. Later they advised my family that I would live, but in all likelihood I would not recover beyond a vegetative state. However, I have in fact advanced far beyond any of their predictions.

It was only after five and a half months in the hospital that I began to slowly realize that I had been seriously and in all likelihood permanently injured. My initial impulse after regaining cognitive control was denial. I recall thinking that my extended stay at the hospital was just some huge joke and I needed to immediately return to my home and job. But I couldn't leave. I was in a hospital bed and couldn't walk. For some unknown reason, I became fixated on escaping from the hospital. I thought that I would wait for an opportune time and crawl out of my hospital room and leave the entire facility. I did this on one occasion and was spotted by hospital staff crawling down the main lobby toward the exit doors. I was quickly returned to my room and tied into bed.

After six months, the physicians at Kentfield concluded that I no longer required around the clock, intense hospital treatment. But I was still severely disabled in many respects, so a less demanding treatment center was medically advised for my care.

I had a great deal of time toward the end of my stay at the Kentfield Rehabilitation Hospital, especially while I was tied in bed, to consider why I was alive on Earth and what I should truly hope to accomplish during my brief existence, an existence that had almost ended a few months earlier. I simply laid in bed pondering this subject, hour after hour. I came to no hard and fast conclusions, but I did have a deep feeling that my lifestyle before July 1, 1995, was missing the real mark. Before my accident I was certainly saving huge corporations large sums of money in civil trials. Nevertheless, while I was lying in bed, staring off into space, I felt that my life could not simply be primarily about economic gain and loss.

Because I had been raised in the Catholic Church, I unquestionably believed in God, Jesus, and the Holy Spirit. But before my accident I never ventured to analyze what their ultimate design was outside of what I heard during sermons at weekly church services. Nonetheless, my mental state on this subject began to stir as a result of my incredibly close encounter with death.

After my sluggish but steady medical improvements, I was released from Kentfield Rehabilitation Hospital and transferred to a rehabilitation center in Berkeley, California, across the San Francisco Bay. The rehabilitation center was not a critical medical care facility. Originally it had actually been a large house in a residential area and was substantially remodeled to include many bedrooms for disabled individuals. Rudimentary medical devices were included in the remodeling in order to meet state requirements.

My stay at the facility is best described as uneventful. Day after day, nothing of any significance occurred. Day and night, using wheelchairs, walkers, or canes, residents would slowly make their way to the living room and watch the same television programs over and over again. There was not much else to do. I could not help but reflect back upon my days as a successful trial attorney. Every day in my legal practice was exciting. I handled cases that, from a monetary standpoint, were huge. I dealt directly with judges and juries. I supervised newer attorneys and staff members in my elaborate and posh office. I also traveled extensively all over the United States as part of my law practice. My stay at the rehabilitation center was exactly the opposite. There I normally remained in my room and did not interact with other residents or watch the unending stream of television programs. As when I was a patient at Kentfield, I spent many of my waking hours considering what was truly the meaning and purpose of my existence on Earth. I was not certain why at the time, but I did feel that being an extremely effective, highly sought-after trial attorney was clearly not the answer. I remained at the Berkeley rehabilitation center for many weeks, deeply involved in this questioning process.

4

Seemingly Endless Recovery

When I finally left the rehabilitation center in Berkeley, I was over-joyed. I had sufficiently recovered to the point that I no longer required rehabilitation center supervision or attention. My recovery had progressed much further than hospital doctors had thought possible. But I do not want to create the misunderstanding that I regained completely normal physical and mental capabilities. I did not. I just no longer required daily medical care and supervision.

While I was in residence at the rehabilitation center, I learned that my wife had been appointed as my legal conservator. I was surprised, because it seemed to me that she had made very infrequent visits to see me. And during those infrequent visits she also appeared to me to be completely caught up in events occurring only in her own life; she was upset with me for damaging our relationship by being involved in the accident. My recollection is that I often told her that I had not planned for a serious accident or lengthy hospitalization to occur, but she persisted with her accusations nonetheless.

Furthermore, I did not understand why I needed a conservator. I had never heard of a legal conservator. I handled civil lawsuits for many rehabilitation centers all over California as part of my employment at Sedgwick, but conservatorship was not a legal relationship that had ever entered into any of my cases. Much to my shock, after doing a bit of legal research at the law library, it became apparent to me that the conservator, my wife, had the legal right to make every decision, even decisions of minimal importance, for the conservatee, namely me. The relationship is usually required only for financial reasons involving gravely ill or dying patients. It seemed immediately obvious to me that my wife did not at that time and would not in the future have my best interests at heart. After I had sufficiently recovered and was able to move out of the rehabilitation center, I asked my wife to legally dissolve the conservatorship, as it made no sense to me. It also made me feel extremely degraded and substantially inferior to ordinary people, in that I couldn't make even the simplest decisions affecting my life. Much to my dismay, my wife flatly refused.

Following my stay at the rehabilitation center, I moved to an apartment in San Rafael, the town in Marin County where I lived before the accident. Compared to the home I occupied before my accident, the apartment was tiny and bare. Nonetheless, my wife had decided that I could not return to residing with her in the home.

Once I'd moved into the apartment, I started what would become a long process of recovery outside of hospitals and rehabilitation facilities. I began to walk again, taking short trips around the apartment with the help of a walker or cane. I also substantially improved my abilities to eat, drink, and prepare simple meals. As my recovery proceeded, I began to feel as though it was necessary to leave the confines of the apartment and walk with a cane outside. During the same time frame, I realized that I would have to accomplish the feat of dressing myself again. For many, many months I had been dressed only in hospital robes and gowns. Dressing myself in pants and shirts was a definite challenge, due to my inability to balance myself. I finally was able to overcome this challenge and developed the aptitude.

Even though it had been nearly a year since my devastating accident, I had almost no ability to speak. Because of my severe brain injury, the words I needed to express myself no longer seemed to exist. Furthermore, one of my vocal cords was permanently paralyzed, and the atrophied muscles in my mouth and jaw caused severe rigidity. This rigidity made me cough a great deal and, much more seriously, resulted in it being inherently difficult to speak.

I went regularly to physical therapy sessions over the next several months to improve my speaking, balance, muscle use, and flexibility. These were primarily offered on an outpatient basis at the Kentfield Rehabilitation Hospital. I made steady, continuous progress as I repeatedly practiced all the techniques back at the apartment where I lived. Despite the exhausting effort this required, I was determined to make as much progress as quickly as I could. Even today, many years later, I remember meeting a judge before whom I had tried several cases. He was also being treated at Kentfield as an outpatient. He told me that of all the other patients he had met at Kentfield and the other facilities where he was treated, I was making by far the fastest and most dramatic improvement. I thanked him sincerely for his comment.

Upon reflection, my motivation for regularly undergoing physical therapy and engaging in efforts to improve my health was completely predictable, given my personality trait of obsession with success. As I stated earlier, I had never been able to stop driving myself. To say that I was generally goal oriented is a vast understatement. I was driven to succeed and always attain my objective. Recovering from my severe injuries was just another objective to which I devoted my time and effort.

While I was struggling to recover, my left eye began drooping uncontrollably. Apparently the back of the eye socket had been smashed during the accident. Reconstructive surgery was performed at Marin General Hospital, and a plastic surgeon removed some of the resulting scar tissue. During this same period, physicians performed facial surgery to attempt to restore my face to normal appearance. A surgeon in a private medical office in Kentfield made several incisions in my lower face and jaw area to improve the bite of my mouth and to enable my chin and jaw to move up and down as I spoke. A surgeon in Larkspur removed facial bones over my left eye and implanted metal straps over and outside of my left eye, because the bones in that area were decomposing. It is ironic to note that before the accident, I was normally a sharply dressed professional with not a hair out of place. Afterward, however, for months and even years, I limped around with a scarred face and visible surgical wounds.

I lived in the apartment in San Rafael for several months. At the beginning, I was visited on almost a daily basis for several hours by three life skills trainers. These life skills trainers were supposed to complete tasks consistent with their job titles. They were remunerated for performing all of the basic chores a severely injured individual needed to subsist: assistance in dressing and bathing, cooking, shopping, cleaning, and so on. Nevertheless, from the very outset of my connection with the life skills trainers, I advised all three of them that they should not do any of these tasks for me. I stressed to them that I could and would fully take care of all my needs to live in the apartment by myself. My attempts were clumsy or awkward, to say the least. By way of example, vacuuming the stairs and the first and second floors was a real adventure, given my almost complete lack of coordination. However, I never seriously hurt myself and managed to perform all of the necessary house-keeping tasks.

I resisted all ordinary assistance from the life skills trainers because I wanted to regain my independence. I had an unquenchable thirst to become completely autonomous once again, just as I was before my accident. The primary manner in which I used the life skills trainers' assistance was to have them take me to my physical therapy and other outpatient treatment sessions. One of the additional consequences of my being involved in the accident and the debilitating injuries was that my driver's license was taken away. Hence I had to rely heavily on the life skills trainers for transportation.

The apartment complex where I resided was located close to a major mall in San Rafael. I lived in the unit alone and usually walked over to the mall to do my shopping, dine at restaurants, and watch movies at the theater. Even though the mall was less than a mile away, when I first started to walk there with a cane, I had to stop and rest periodically or hold onto trees for balance as I passed them. After a few weeks, I began a new and more intense physical recovery regimen. I no longer used a cane to assist me to walk, so I disposed of it. I walked to a nearby high school and limped around the track, stopping periodically to regain my balance. I did this at least three times a week. I also began reading intensely a variety of different books. I purchased a computer to install in my apartment and relearned how to type and use many of the programs.

I also looked at the local junior college's list of classes and registered for two courses that were offered that semester, the fall of 1997. I took a couple of business courses. Both courses were fun, and it was gratifying to be involved in the academic learning process again. Nonetheless, I was significantly older than most of the other students in the classes, and my disabilities were outwardly obvious. One of the classrooms, for example, had a series of steps that students had to ascend to get to the rows of seats. For me to accomplish such a climb, I had to bend over and carefully hold onto seats to balance me as I was moving up to the higher levels of seating. Moreover, whenever I opened my mouth and began responding to the teacher or talking in any way, it was instantly obvious to everyone in the classroom that I had a severe speech disability.

The entire time I remained in the apartment in San Rafael, I diligently followed my physical exercise regimen. I never missed my routine of walking the track three times a week. By this point I had developed the ability to walk or limp quickly and would spend long periods roaming the streets in San Rafael. I also engaged in daily speech exercises that I had learned from one of my speech therapists. My ability to speak to others had improved but was still far from normal.

After a few months, I thought my improvement was quite substantial, under the circumstances. I pointed this out to my wife, who was still my legal conservator. I told her how offended I felt by the entire process and that I certainly believed it was no longer necessary. I asked her once again to dissolve the conservatorship. Again, she flatly refused my request. Therefore I thought I had no recourse but to hire attorneys who would move to set aside the conservatorship on my behalf. This was an area of law that I knew nothing about, and I still had many physical and mental deficiencies.

When my wife found out that I had retained an attorney to legally challenge the conservatorship, without delay she hired several attorneys to frustrate my efforts. It took several weeks and a great deal of attorney time to prepare legal documents and respond to discovery, but the motion to dissolve the conservatorship was finally heard by a court of law. I prevailed against her and no longer had a legal conservator.

The court ruling had a monumental effect on me, both mentally and emotionally. In the legal sense, I no longer felt as though I was a small child whose every important decision had to be made by a ruling parent. Before the conservatorship was dissolved, I had been under my wife's complete control. I felt as if I had to follow all her commands, whether I agreed with them or not. In my opinion, her overwhelming motivation was to improve her financial position at my expense. Shortly after the conservatorship motion was heard, my wife filed for legal separation. Additional events occurred that resulted in our divorce a few months after the conservatorship motion was decided. We no longer have any relationship whatsoever.

By contrast, the relationships I had with my mother and older brother during this time period were remarkably diverse to me. Both my mother and brother visited me frequently throughout my hospitalizations and during my intense recovery periods. My mother was always optimistic and encouraging. She often remarked that I had made so much progress in so many areas, that I should certainly not give up my efforts. I should continue on with my efforts in every respect. My brother was employed full time in a very demanding occupation. Nevertheless, he somehow made the time to visit me during my ongoing medical treatment. Moreover, like my mother, he was very encouraging.

All of the attorney friends I had before the accident largely vanished. They were generally too busy with their careers and other activities to maintain an active friendship with someone as disabled as me. At first I felt very much alone. I felt as though I was no longer an individual who interested these very successful individuals. I felt despair. I felt that because I no longer had a career on the forefront of the legal world in the United States, I could no longer capture their attention.

My mother and brother largely took the place of my former friends and interacted with me in a variety of ways. I went out to restaurants with them. I rode with them in their vehicles to explore various locales along the California coastline and in more remote areas of Marin County. I often visited them at their homes, and we engaged in a host of entertaining activities. I would have spent my time during the first few months after the accident almost entirely alone if it had not been for them. They were extremely generous with their time and inordinately supportive. My relationships with them have remained extremely close during the years that have passed since the accident.

After successfully dissolving the conservatorship, I used what money I had saved and purchased a home in Novato, California. Novato is still in Marin County, but it's a few miles north of San Rafael. I made the purchase in 1997 and moved to the house alone. In my house in Novato, I continued with my physical and speech exercise routines. I incorporated a weight lifting schedule as well, since I had lifted weights periodically during the previous twenty years. My participation in the two junior college courses was also still somewhat time consuming. Moreover, I began reading books and studying subjects on the Internet a substantial amount of time each day.

What remained very inconvenient was vehicular transportation. I was physically able to leave my house whenever I desired, but to get to places I had to rely on my mother or brother, or take public transportation such as buses. I had driven a car myself for many years prior to the accident. And although I lost my driver's license as a result of my accident, it seemed to me that I was now physically and mentally capable of operating a motor vehicle once again. So I went to the local Department of Motor Vehicles and obtained information about what would be on the driver's license test. I also had a vehicle left over from my pre-accident days, and I used it to practice driving in off-road locations. Then I took the written and driving tests administered by the Department of Motor Vehicles. I passed each test easily. Much to my delight, I could again transport myself to different locations by using a car.

At this point in my life, I still had a severe speech impairment. People could generally understand about half of the words I spoke. Additionally, my coordination had not greatly improved. I continued to have to hold onto various objects as I passed by or stop completely in order to steady my gait. Moreover, even though I walked fast in my unstable way for long distances, I was and still am completely unable to accelerate into a run.

Emotionally, I felt as if I were existing in a vacuum. I was slowly yet steadily overcoming my disabilities. Although I did not believe that my disabilities were responsible, I felt as though I was not really achieving my destiny or calling in life. As a result, I began fixating upon my weekly church visits. I was born and raised a Catholic and attended Catholic school up to and including part of my ninth grade year. I had attended mass every Sunday my entire life with very few exceptions, such as when I was traveling in third-world countries. In the late 1990s I strongly focused on my church attendance and began reading the Bible and a number of books discussing the relationship between God and mankind. Yet my queries and frequent church visits did not resolve my repeated inquiries. I felt as if my fate was to establish a personal relationship with God here and now. I fervently believed that I should and must acknowledge God in the present and not focus primarily on events that had occurred in the distant past.

5

Beginning to Awaken to Reality

Once, in the middle of the night, I awoke with a multitude of thoughts about mankind's existence on Earth. I had been contemplating this topic almost daily since my brush with death on June 30, 1995. This particular night, though, my reflections were different. After many months, it seemed to me that I had awakened with some answers.

Even though I had been considering this subject for many months, it still seemed unlikely that someone with my background would formulate these somewhat unusual ideas. My primary experiences in life had been in the areas of law, business, and construction, but the answers that appeared in my mind that night dealt with theology, the study of God. These concepts kept reverberating in my thoughts, and while this was occurring, I had another idea. I thought maybe, just maybe, I had established some type of connection with the Almighty, and God was advising me of crucial matters involving my existence. I thought this was logical and sensible, given my near-death experience and almost constant pondering of the subject. I also speculated that since the areas discussed in the documents I wrote and now set forth in this book were so remote to me, I must have had some external input to even come up with the subjects. That input may have been directly from God.

That night I felt as though I had begun to awaken to reality. Even though it was very late, I could no longer sleep. I felt impelled to type out my thoughts about the Creator:

The Creator

How and why was the universe created? What other entities are there in the universe? What is mankind's purpose on Earth? Are there several different dimensions and hence completely different universes and levels of existence?

These questions are incredibly complex. To answer any but the most basic inquiries far exceeds mankind's ability. Mankind is thousands of years old, and science has progressed a great deal, but human beings have only the most rudimentary understanding of the complexities of existence.

It is clearly impossible for any human being to know with certainty the answers to any of these questions, or even to be definitely aware of the reasons why human beings exist on Earth and why we are so different from and superior to every other creature on this planet.

Precisely because mankind is unable to explain any but the most basic tenets of existence, human beings have formed and participated in religions. Although religions differ in every major society on Earth, they were constructed by human beings to provide differing measures of comfort and knowledge for those who participate.

Religion is a set of beliefs held by a distinct social class or particular group of people concerning the meaning and purpose of existence. An almost infinite number of additional questions emanate from this initial point of inquiry. However, the answers to many of these queries are based wholly on a belief system. Mankind is unable to do otherwise in light of the current state of human knowledge.

Whether they are aware of it or not, most human beings on Earth entertain some form of belief about the meaning and purpose of existence. Even atheists have considered the matter and have arrived at some conclusions as to why the presence of a god or gods does not make sense in the timeless grand scheme of events.

For my part, I am just one of the tens of billions of human beings who have existed on Earth. I was raised in a certain country, in a specific lifestyle; I was brought up in particular social groups. To a large extent, I am a function of the time in which I was born, the nation and locale in which I was raised, and my exposure through books, lectures, and conversations with other people concerning their thoughts and ideas.

The major element that makes me dramatically different from other individuals is that I have a mind of my own. Even though my mental framework is to some extent governed by my upbringing, my education, my experience, and my interaction with others, I still have the ability to engage in independent thought. Everyone does. But the extent to which they actually do so depends completely on the person.

Based on all these governing factors and my own independent thought, I have developed my own explanation for creation. Since it is clearly impossible for any human being to develop such an explanation based upon fact, mine is likewise based on a series of beliefs. As might be expected, my beliefs are grounded in my upbringing, education, experience, and interaction with others, and in my own thoughts. My beliefs are also premised on my nearly fatal accident, my continuous consideration of the topic, and most importantly, my interaction with the Almighty.

It is completely obvious to me that the universe, in general, and the Earth, in particular, had to have been created. They simply would not be in existence without some entity willing them into existence. The universe is complicated, far beyond human understanding. Even the Earth alone staggers the human imagination. Therefore, some entity had to intend for all this to be formed and ultimately exist at the time of creation. The majority of human beings have believed that the creator is God or several different gods. My own personal beliefs are as follows.

I believe in the one, true God. I believe that Jesus Christ was also the Almighty in different form and came down to Earth to redeem mankind. I also believe in the Holy Spirit.

One of the basic foundations of Christian religions, which I think is so fundamentally important, is that all people, irrespective of age, culture, society, race, or gender, are judged, in part, by how they helped or assisted other human beings. In my interpretation, the Bible, the Ten Commandments, and even Jesus's life here on Earth, all largely stand for the proposition that we, as human beings, need to consistently help one another. It is largely because I totally and completely agree with this basic principle that I find and experience such a oneness with and sense of belonging in Christ's teachings.

But one critically important aspect should never be forgotten. Religion is a term used to designate a social or cultural group's interaction with God. It is fine for that society and people to operate largely through social or cultural groups. No one should ever overlook, however, that their relationship with God is a personal and timeless one.

You are born alone. You will die alone. And you will enter into the life hereafter alone. You will always share every aspect of your existence with one nonhuman entity. That entity is God. It cannot be overemphasized how critically important this level of understanding is for every person that lives on Earth.

After I wrote this document over the course of several days and nights, I spent more time considering other aspects of our lives here on Earth. I continued periodically waking up in the middle of the night, thinking that I had been directly communicating with God. The next document that I wrote is titled "Inescapable Conclusions."

Inescapable Conclusions

The all-encompassing, primary conclusion that every human being should reach, irrespective of when or where they were born, is that God created the Earth, all of the flora and fauna therein, and all human life. One thing that many of us often overlook is that God has a personal, individual relationship with each of us. The time or place of our birth, life, and death does not matter. It also does not matter if we do not understand how God can have individual relationships with each one of us when God is a single entity. It is enough to realize only that this entity is the *all-powerful God*. We are just simple human beings and probably do not understand more than a fraction of the wonderful concepts of heaven, eternity, or unceasing goodness.

A related inescapable conclusion is that we should not focus to an improper extent on the worldly gifts and attributes we acquire during our lives here on Earth. All people need to fully realize that material possessions, money, and even their physical attributes mean absolutely nothing unless they are used to conform with God's laws and teachings.

Everyone should realize that people should use their natural and inherent gifts and abilities to worship God, sanctify their lives, and assist other truly needy people when opportunities present themselves. To use our abilities solely to further our own personal needs and desires is often merely selfish.

What should also never be overlooked is that how we prepare for and pursue a career or occupation may have a tumultuous effect on our lives. Preparation for a career includes education, skills, work experience, life background, and establishing relations with people already in the field. Depending on the job, a person may have a great deal of specific abilities necessary for the occupation before entering the position. It completely depends on the individual and the particular career.

People do not expend all their time in careers or occupations. They also engage in numerous personal interests such as family, social activities, and hobbies. These can be the most highly rewarding experiences for people, depending on how they spend their spare time. Unfortunately, some individuals completely abuse their allocations of free time. Instead of spending it in useful ways, they use their time in completely selfish, self-absorbed ways. Examples of such behavior include drug use, excessive alcohol consumption, stealing, and injuring others.

We should all recognize that our activities during the brief period we are on Earth may impact how and where we will spend eternity according to God's plans and directives. We should clearly analyze the possible ramifications of the decisions we make during our lives on this planet. We should carefully and thoughtfully evaluate what possible effect our decisions will have on ourselves and others, both now and forever.

After writing this document, I began to form a substantial number of additional mental impressions concerning God and what we were all placed on Earth to accomplish. To be candid, I could not help but feel that my new habit of arising in the middle of the night every few days with such thoughts was unusual, if not bizarre. Nevertheless, because I considered these thoughts to be so central to mankind's existence here on Earth, I continued the practice of typing these small treatises. The next one I prepared was titled "The Clarity of Human Existence."

The Clarity of Human Existence

Was all of humanity placed on Earth to exercise power over one another? Is the reason for living life to accumulate wealth? Or is it to form a score of sensual relationships? Maybe it is to succeed in life through self-serving employment objectives. Or perhaps humanity's function on Earth is simply to achieve self-gratification, regardless of the cost to other human beings.

In my opinion, these are extremely myopic and selfish views. I also believe they fail to focus on God's overall objective in forming mankind and placing us here on Earth to exist individually for a brief time.

It should be apparent that every life form on Earth is extremely complicated. Whether it is plants, insects, fish, reptiles, or mammals, their inherent natures are complex. Moreover, our tremendous mental capabilities still far exceed our complete scientific understanding.

The inquiry is on a much more magnificent scale than just these concepts. The weather, the land masses, the oceans, and the forces and dimensions that govern life here on Earth are so amazingly well formulated that it staggers the imagination. And when the configurations of Earth, the galaxy, and the entire universe are considered, it is completely awe inspiring. It should be fundamentally obvious that all these must have been created by an all-powerful, timeless entity. That entity is God. The totality of God's existence is far too complex for human beings to even begin to understand. Nonetheless, that is not necessary. Because of this inability, human beings have formed many major world religions to interact with God. These religions have also been developed to devise belief systems concerning divine intentions. Furthermore, God has frequently interacted with people here on Earth. This has occurred through the Almighty's exchanges with various human beings; various forms of literature, including the Bible; and Jesus's life here on Earth.

I am now stating my own beliefs, as it is literally impossible to substantiate my thoughts regarding God. I believe that God interacts with other entities for some purpose or reason. I think that is why God created angels. In my opinion, angels are far superior to human beings. Obviously, they exist in a different environment than humanity and may even live eternally in a different universe or realm of reality. God created angels with a free will. According to various church teachings, some angels rebelled against God. These same church teachings emphasize that such angels no longer exist in heaven with God.

Human beings clearly need to interact with one another out of necessity. That is why families live together and people coexist in communities, cities, and nations.

It should never be forgotten or downplayed that God shared with humanity how they should live their temporary lives here on Earth. Human beings should love, honor, and respect God. Furthermore, all people should act unselfishly and come to others' assistance when the reasonable opportunity arises.

It was uncanny how I began intensely considering these religious topics suddenly and only after my accident. Before that calamity, I only superficially listened to sermons delivered at mass and never really analyzed the messages conveyed in any detail. After surviving the accident and enduring of the slow process of recovery, I believed I was finally beginning to understand the actual nature of reality. It was almost as if I was born again, but this time with a focus and an expanded comprehension of the true nature of life on Earth.

I determined then that my understanding could and should be magnified by reading and taking notes on various books like the Holy Bible, treatises on the world's major religions, and scientific textbooks on physics and astronomy.

Not long after I began this mental journey, however, one theme kept reappearing in my mind. I kept wondering why it was that God would have anything to do with such fragile, simplistic, and fleeting entities as human beings. I kept thinking in particular that Christian religions advance the doctrine that we are all God's children. How could this be?

After some consideration, I came up with the only answer that made sense to me. The answer is contained in the following document:

How Can We Be God's Children?

In the multitude of religions on earth that believe in God, it is stated over and over again that human beings are God's children. This statement is often repeated, but rarely evaluated.

Analysis of the concept overwhelms the imagination. God is the Creator of all. God created heaven and Earth and an unlimited number of planets, galaxies, and the universe or universes. God created the forces and dimensions that govern how the planets interact with one another and how life on Earth is able to survive.

God is eternal and not subject to the dimension of time. God had no beginning and will have no end. God is all-powerful. God's abilities are so unlimited that we, as human beings, cannot even begin to understand what God is capable of doing. God is all-knowing. Again, we as human beings cannot even begin to understand the awareness of God.

The eminently logical question that immediately flows from this inquiry is the following: How can rudimentary, frail, and ephemeral human beings ever be considered, in any sense whatsoever, children of the Creator? How can human beings ever even imagine that there is any basis for believing that they are God's children?

In my opinion, it is because of one factor and one factor alone: God is also all *good*. God is a completely holy entity. God's creative abilities far exceed human understanding and always will. But what human beings are capable of understanding is that they, too, can act as good, honest, caring, and generous people. This is the crucial element humanity can and often does have in common with God. Again, in my opinion, this is precisely why human beings are able to consider themselves God's children.

It is also my belief that mankind's ability to be kind, to be charitable, and to be moral are not related to a person's location or place in history at all. Humanity does not naturally advance or retreat in this capability with the passage of time. Moreover, mankind's scientific and technical advances are completely unrelated to people's ethical nature.

It is undeniable that God has encouraged human beings always to act with integrity. When God gave Moses the Ten Commandments, it became abundantly clear that people should act toward one another in a manner consistent with the written tablets Moses carried down from Mt. Sinai. The entire Old Testament contains various communications from God, primarily to the ancient Jews, directing them to lead caring and unselfish lives. God's message to humanity was greatly amplified by Jesus's life here on Earth. Jesus taught that human beings should not harm one another in thought, word, or deed. Jesus did not teach people here on Earth how to advance scientifically or technologically. Jesus did instruct scores of people, however, how to advance ethically. Jesus did this both verbally and, more importantly, through his example.

The major religions of the world do not teach that people ought to further themselves economically, politically, or technologically. But like the divine instructions, they do teach that people ought to become more honest, caring, and generous.

If we truly are God's children, I then asked, how is it possible, given the huge and almost limitless diversity in people's backgrounds and behaviors, that the ultimate choice between heaven and hell can motivate the ethical choices of all humanity? How, given the actions advocated by different governments, societies, churches, and other individuals, can all people come to understand that morality and the concepts of good and evil govern where they will go after life here on Earth? These thought processes caused me to formulate additional opinions and prepare the following document:

Endless Speculation

Mankind's speculation is timeless and almost limitless. During the existence of humanity on Earth, many individuals have speculated about why they truly exist and how and what they are supposed to achieve during their brief lifetimes. Indeed, people have become immersed in a myriad of conjectures concerning what should be accomplished during life. This topic has been the subject of innumerable books, articles, lectures, sermons, and other forms of communications.

A multitude of formal religions have been created by human beings. Morality and ethics have been advocated by a wide variety of different human institutions and organizations.

Unfortunately, wars have even been justified as consistent with God's ideals. Unmitigated violence, assault, and conversion of property all have historically been perpetrated by people claiming to be committing those atrocities in God's name. In my opinion, nothing could be further from the truth.

It should never be downplayed or overlooked that people provide their own interpretations and beliefs as to what God espouses. Those conceptions are the direct thinking of human beings. We have only limited glimpses and segments of what God actually thinks of how people should interact with one another.

The relationship between mankind and God and, more directly, the manner in which human beings relate to one another are guided by individual experiences, attributes, and motivations. People's relationships with God and with one another vary tremendously. The manner in which individuals act toward others ordinarily varies widely, depending upon age, gender, lifestyle, religious affinity, social interaction, type of employment, education, interests, mannerisms, hobbies, and so on.

In my opinion, the reason why our ability to interact with God and others is so markedly variable is because God endowed all human beings with a free will. This substantiates the notion that the life human beings live on Earth is largely a *test* to determine whether they will be elevated to a higher level after the test is completed. All of the major Christian religions espouse the belief that if human beings pass the test, they will be elevated to heaven. Other non-Christian religions may not share the concept of heaven, but they often do stress that life after death continues in another form of sublime existence. It is my belief that what we imagine as the form of life after death cannot ever be anything but absolute speculation based upon religious values. From a pure logical standpoint, however, the concept of elevation to heaven, and only to heaven, if the test is passed is difficult to comprehend.

God's knowledge, power, and abilities are limitless. That God is able to judge all human lives here on Earth clearly exceeds the grasp of the human mind. One cannot even begin to understand how such a monumental task can be performed. One cannot help but wonder, however, what will happen to the vast number of people who have been only marginally decent persons and whose egocentric conduct harmed others, even if they may not have purposely intended to cause harm.

If God is all-forgiving, will those people be elevated to heavenly status? Furthermore, if God is all-forgiving, will all people, regardless of how they conducted their lives here on Earth, be elevated to heaven after their demise?

It is my conviction that such thinking bespeaks an important confusion of terms. Unquestionably, God is all-forgiving. But this tenet means exactly what the words state: if an individual commits countless serious sins against the Almighty and other individuals during their life on Earth, God will forgive them. *Nevertheless*, this does not mean they will be elevated to heaven. God is perfect in every respect. Unquestionably, God has the ability, and exercises that ability, to forgive every person of their sins. Determining whether the individual is worthy of joining God in heaven, however, is a completely different matter. We should never forget that.

Why should habitual sinners get the opportunity to spend eternity in paradise? What may make more sense, given our innumerably varied situations, is that there may be various intermediate levels or layers of existence that people will experience after they expire on Earth but before they are elevated to heaven.

The universe is probably infinite in size. There may be an unlimited number of universes that exist. Thus the locales in which individual souls can exist is limitless. Since God's powers have no confines, why is it necessary to limit the answer to only *one* outcome for the question of whether a person is worthy of being elevated to heaven? Why not have the examination continue at several different layers or levels? This is simply a question posed for further consideration.

At first, especially when I was painstakingly reviewing the Holy Bible, I kept thinking about life some two thousand years ago and halfway around the world. As I prepared the documents incorporated into this book, my thoughts turned to the here and now. It seems to me that it is much more meaningful to determine how to act in a manner consistent with God's teachings presently than to focus only or to an extreme on what happened a great number of years ago in a remote part of the world.

Shortly, after I had these thoughts, I woke up again in the middle of the night and prepared the following document:

Temptation

Human existence at the present time is very disparate, depending upon the country in which an individual resides. Arguably, the United States is currently at an economic, military, and technological climax.

As a result of many decades of hard work and careful planning and organizing, Americans live in a society and culture where most goods and services are available. In fact, many Americans are so economically well off, they can afford to pay for very expensive products and services. Most Americans primarily determine whether to purchase a good or request a service based on whether they can afford the item or service and sometimes on whether it is legal to do so. A significant number of Americans are not restrained by either consideration.

This entire process is complicated by the social norms and standards prevailing in this country. American society often condones individual conduct that is contrary to God's teachings. A large number of Americans are centrally involved in such activities. These individuals exercise their free will and determine that the rewards of their activities, which are often mainly monetary, outweigh the moral implications.

It is easy to condemn the serious illegal activities. These include murder, kidnapping, rape, robbery, and other severe crimes. It is simple to condemn such crimes because it is patently obvious that the individual committing the crimes acutely injures others. Illegal activities that do not immediately or seriously injure others are often more difficult to rigidly condemn. These involve selling some of the less addictive unlawful drugs, selling alcohol to intoxicated individuals or underage minors, petty theft, prostitution, and other less severe crimes.

The legal and socially acceptable activities that result in individuals not blatantly harming themselves or others are even more difficult to judge. These include drinking alcohol to excess, engaging in adultery, lying, cheating, taking property from a family member or friend, watching pornography, and so on. The overriding reason why it is so difficult to always condemn these forms of conduct is that often it is not absolutely certain that anyone else will be harmed by such conduct. Moreover, people on the outside never know all or often not even most of the circumstances motivating such conduct. Such conduct may possibly damage the person committing the acts and may damage others mentally or physically, but may also, depending on the circumstances, be arguably justifiable.

In America today, there are many legally permissible situations in which people can engage in the conduct described above, particularly as described in the preceding paragraph. Under current social norms and standards, there are almost an unlimited number of temptations that confront individuals.

One way to refrain from engaging in those activities is to avoid such tempting situations altogether whenever possible.

More importantly, it has been my experience that people need to constantly ask whether their conduct will harm others. It may not hurt other people who are directly involved, but it may seriously injure others who are peripherally involved.

My inquiries into the paramount issues affecting human existence continued. At first it seemed strange to me that I kept waking up at odd hours of the night, every week or two, with what seemed like answers to my inquiries. I then felt compelled to write out my thoughts on paper. At the time, I was not certain what I would do with these documents other than keep them in my filing cabinet. But over time it became clear to me that I wanted to share with other people the effect that the accident had had on me and my way of thinking. Until recently I was not certain how I would accomplish that goal. It is my hope that I am now achieving that goal with this book.

6

Performing Volunteer Work

As my awakening to reality began, my life underwent some monumental changes. As I pondered my newly formulated thoughts on what really mattered in my existence, it dawned on me that I no longer needed to live in the San Francisco Bay Area. I was no longer employed in San Francisco as a civil trial attorney, after all, and after my motorcycle accident I was incapable of performing the duties of that job.

I loved to travel and had done a great deal of exploring around the United States and also the world. But I definitely wanted to remain in the United States, because I believed that it was a marvelous place to live in terms of its political and economic systems, its technological capabilities, and its standard of living. Of all the states that I had visited, the most spellbinding for its beauty and serenity was Hawaii. Therefore, I moved there.

After moving to Hawaii, I continued to consider what life was truly about and what I should endeavor to accomplish during my brief existence on this planet. I was aware that I would probably spend the rest of my life recovering from my seriously debilitating physical injuries. Although this clearly did not prevent me from assisting others, it meant that the kind of assistance I could provide would be a bit unusual, given my rather limited abilities and physical infirmities.

The individuals I encountered through the volunteer work in which I became involved would be aware of such infirmities immediately upon meeting me. I still had many scars on my head and other parts of my body. I continued to have a speech deficit, which prevented many people from understanding even the majority of what I said. And my equilibrium persisted in being far from normal.

Nevertheless, it was apparent to me that I could still assist truly needy individuals. Therefore, shortly after moving to Hawaii, I reflected a great deal on the subject of helping other people. This thinking led me to write three documents on the subjects of neighborly love, the golden rule, and selfless existence.

Love Your Neighbor as Yourself

Over the history of human civilization, there have been many different cultures and societies. There have also been a host of different faiths or religions. Historically, the form of religion complemented the culture or society involved, at least initially. This relation was necessary. In order for the overall concepts of the meaning and purpose of life here on Earth to appear meaningful, they had to be translated into forms consistent with local customs and practices.

It is a fact of human history that the vast majority of faiths had their origins in Asia: Hinduism, Buddhism, Jainism, and Sikhism in India; Confucianism and Taoism in China; Zoroastrianism in Iran; Judaism and Christianity in Palestine (now Israel); and Islam in Arabia. Over time, each of the major faiths has expanded to different locations on the planet.

Even within a specific faith or religion, there are significant variations in beliefs between members, based upon their educational, employment, and economic backgrounds as well as their real-life experiences. In fact, everyone's determination concerning the purpose for their existence on Earth is an entirely personal endeavor.

All of the major religions have one crucial aspect in common, which should never be downplayed in the quest for existential meaning: they all fervently promote being a loving, caring, kind, and generous person. They unequivocally encourage all people to give part of their time, resources, efforts, and energy to assist or help others who are less fortunate.

What is the position of the five major religions—Christianity, Judaism, Buddhism, Islam, and Hinduism—on this subject?

The central figure in the entire analysis of Christianity is Jesus. He was a compassionate and kind teacher and orator. He led by his example. He also fully accepted all people, irrespective of race, gender, or nationality. On one particularly momentous occasion, Jesus said one of the most important commandments is "Love your neighbor as yourself." Jesus frequently referred to himself as the Son of Man. His disciples more often referred to him as the Son of God. He was more than simply a messiah. God alone was capable of forgiving the sins of mankind. By his death of the cross, Jesus eradicated the sins of mankind.

Judaism encompasses many groups of people, including religious worshippers, secular groups, and Zionists. Jewish tradition teaches that God gave Moses the five books of the Torah. Also important to the Jewish tradition is the Talmud, which preserves the ancient oral tradition of rabbinical law in the Mishnah, and later commentary on the Mishnah in the Gemara. Two of the most memorable statements in the Mishnah are:

"All is foreseen, but free choice is granted. The world is judged with mercy and all is measured by the number of good deeds."

"Who is wise? He who learns from every man. Who is strong? He who controls his passions. Who is rich? He who is happy with his portion. Who is honorable? He who honors his fellow men."

The Buddhist teachings are vast and complex. Buddhism originated in India and has been accepted by people in many other countries. The core figure in the Buddhist tradition is Gautama Buddha. He was born in Lumbini near the Indian border with Nepal sometime between 563 and 483 BCE. Gautama Buddha did not ask the people to accept his teachings simply because it was the word of the Buddha. He invited them to understand and practice the teachings and realize the truth for themselves. To attain enlightenment and progress on the Buddhist path, there are six Paramitas, or perfections, that individuals should practice and repeatedly perform: (1) generosity, (2) moral discipline, (3) patience, (4) energy, (5) meditation, and (6) wisdom.

The people who practice Islam are of many different nationalities and cultures. They submit to one God, however, and follow the message of the Prophet Muhammad. Muhammad was born in the town of Mecca in Arabia in the year 570 CE. The main source of Islamic law is the Qur'an, which is the word of God as revealed to the Prophet Muhammad. Islam emphasizes that all people are equal. Islam also stresses the moral value of each action and makes morality the basis of salvation. The Prophet Muhammad made it abundantly clear that Islam is built upon many pillars. One of the primary pillars is to assist others, whether Muslim or non-Muslim.

Hinduism is defined by neither an exclusive, authoritative scripture nor an established church. The central Hindu doctrine is that God can be understood as the indescribable Supreme Being or Braham. The ultimate aim of Hindus is to attain salvation (moksha), which is to attain union with God. In order to achieve *moksha*, man has to free himself from the chain of births and deaths. The duties and responsibilities of an individual are termed *karma*. One important precept of Hinduism is that you must respect your mother, your father, your teacher, and your guest. Hindus believe that one should try to find God within the heart of every being.

Even a cursory study confirms that people have worshipped God in a host of distinct ways at different times and places. Not only are there many formal, established religions, but also there are almost an unlimited number of individual relationships with the divine Creator. That only one formal religion is the correct one appears entirely unlikely.

It is my determined conclusion that God established humanity for a specific purpose. I believe God performed this miracle of creation in order to witness human beings nurturing and caring for one another. This ideal is confirmed in the Ten Commandments, which primarily set forth how people should relate to one another.

The scriptures and teachings of the many different established religions specify in detail what is good and bad conduct. All the major religions make it abundantly clear that assisting or helping out your fellow man is a wonderful way to live your life here on Earth. Conversely, harming other individuals or being involved in selfish endeavors only to gratify personal desires is ordinarily regarded as negative conduct.

It is critically important at this juncture to set forth my own personal beliefs concerning how all of us who have ever lived on Earth are going to be judged in the hereafter. I believe everyone's judgment will be based to varying extents on when and where they existed. People may have spent their entire lifetime in harsh surroundings or in relative comfort, or in any number of alternative situations. I believe that all will be considered when we are judged.

I do not believe that anyone must believe in the existence of Jesus, Moses, Buddha, Muhammad, or any other individual that existed on Earth. Given the era, location, and circumstances under which the person lived his or her life here on Earth, he or she may be familiar with some or all of the above individuals, but I do not consider it essential. All of these individuals unquestionably led loving, caring, generous lives. They provided many of us with wonderful examples of how to live life, but again, if a person was not fortunate enough during their brief lifetime to hear about these individuals, I do not consider that to be an essential loss.

Perhaps even more unsettling is my faith that even a belief in God is not an absolute necessity. Once again, I think one's belief in God depends on the era, location, and circumstances surrounding the person's life here on Earth. It would be a tragedy to conclude that just because a person died at an early age or lived life in an area where it was not accepted that God was the creator of human existence, he or she will not be allowed to go to heaven. I believe that such thoughts defy logic and that God would never act in such an unsubstantiated, random fashion.

This leads to my final belief regarding the meaning and purpose of life, a belief that is consistent with the teachings of all the major established religions in the world. My belief is that it is fundamental for all individuals to be loving, caring, honest, generous, and helpful human beings.

Foundation of the Golden Rule

Why are we alive? What are our goals, aspirations, and purposes in life? What are we going to accomplish during our lifetimes?

Are we going to excel in business, law, medicine, science, construction, or sports to the degree that we achieve notoriety and fame in our lives? Are we going to become wealthy and acquire most, if not all, of the lavish worldly possessions?

Or is our focus in life different? Are we determined to make a significant contribution? In essence, will we use our background, education, skills, abilities, and experience to often assist or help other people?

Many people fail to consider the notion that God created humanity for a definite purpose. What should never be de-emphasized is that God has a specific reason for every person's individual existence. People often set goals and objectives that are not consistent with God's overall plan. Such individuals will have to deal with God in the afterlife, especially if such inconsistencies occur for only selfish reasons.

Jesus set down a wonderful example for us. He spent his entire adult life helping others. Many people ignore this clear and direct message and simply focus on self-necessitated worldly possessions, status, and monetary rewards to enrich their lives.

Jesus did not sacrifice his life on the cross to enable just a segment of the population to enjoy wealth and a prosperous life here on Earth. Jesus died and was reborn to redeem all of us from our sins. In essence, he did this to give us all an opportunity to enjoy an eternal existence in heaven.

Whether or not we share eternal existence in heaven with Jesus completely depends on how we determine to live during our limited time on the planet. In other words, are we willing to support God's plan or will we reject it?

God's plan requires individual human recognition and genuine involvement in his divine purpose. Recognition means faith, hope, and belief. Genuine involvement means, in essence, placing your faith, hope, and belief into action by actually providing personal service or assistance to other truly needy human beings.

Unquestionably, recognition is important. People must have the right ideals and beliefs. Nevertheless, involvement is the crucial element. In my view, people cannot simply think they ought to be acting correctly. In the grand scheme of things, they *must* actually act beneficially.

God has given humanity details concerning satisfactory conduct. The most noteworthy description was set forth during Jesus's life on Earth. One point that Jesus stressed over and over again, which is known as the Golden Rule, states "You shall love your neighbor as yourself." This doctrine is completely straightforward. People should never harm or mistreat other individuals. Also critically important and often overlooked is that people should assist or help other individuals when it is feasible to do so and when the assistance will not be abused or misused.

It is my belief that these doctrines are the cornerstones for all of humankind's existence. However, human beings have a free will. It is up to us entirely whether we choose to accept or reject them.

Selfless Existence

Since the dawn of civilization, many human beings have too often focused excessively on themselves. People are tempted to indulge in both physical and mental forms of self-gratification. Such motivations are ordinarily selfish. There are also people in the world who strive to attain the opposite of a selfish existence. These people attempt to achieve a selfless way of life. Some of the activities they engage in to become selfless include the following:

- Obtaining material possessions to help their fellow man.

- Becoming involved in a career or employment endeavor principally to make a difference in the society in which they live.

- Achieving a high social status in order to become a fine leader and role model and to guide associates to work responsibly and wisely.

- Associating with and having concern for people who are needy, elderly, sick, or poverty stricken and assisting them in order to lighten their burdens.

- Donating food to the hungry.

- Remaining alcohol and drug free for the sake of being an excellent role model to children and other adults.

- Taking good care of their own health, in turn, so they will be able to continue assisting their fellow man.

- Dressing modestly as a way of being respectful.

- Assisting relatives and friends in their domestic responsibilities.

- Teaching children and others by their own straightforward examples.

- Helping others in their employment efforts.

- Directing others to the appropriate governmental and private agencies that can help them fulfill their needs.

- Assisting organizations by maintaining or improving places of employment or individual work spaces.

- Providing counseling to others in areas in which they have developed expertise.

- Interacting continuously with God, who guides them in unlimited, wonderful ways.

This list continues almost boundlessly.

People should never overlook the fact that acquiring physical possessions primarily to satisfy their own egos is selfish. By measuring their success through the number and costliness of their physical possessions, they may feel as though they have accomplished a great deal during their lives. The emptiness of such a belief system is dramatically borne out by the fact that none of these physical possessions will accompany them after they die.

It cannot be emphasized too dramatically that all people are here on earth briefly. Initially, we are all children. Then we become adults. Lastly, we enter our elderly years. As we pass through these phases, we should never forget that life passes more rapidly as we age.

Our lives are spent with a variety of different ideas and attitudes. Unequivocally though, life is simply a transitory passage of time. All of us need to focus on meaningful aspects of what we have learned during our brief existence on Earth to set the stage for life after death. In all likelihood, if we live largely selfless lives, helping and assisting others, our benefits will be eternal.

If, on the other hand, we live selfish, self-centered lives, then God will reward us accordingly. Without even considering the ramifications of what Jesus Christ taught, everyone must see that it is eminently sensible and fulfilling to be honest, caring, and generous.

At this point, the uncommon and unconventional nature of my thought processes became abundantly apparent to me. I was not writing these documents for any established religion. I was not regurgitating or restating any accepted formal religious doctrine. I had reviewed many different publications pertaining to a considerable number of world religions, but my thoughts did not mirror any specific religion. My thoughts came to me independently, in the middle of many nights. It is my judgment that the thoughts that came to me were divinely inspired.

I continued to ponder what actual opportunities there were for me to assist other truly needy individuals, given my background and limitations. I was determined to go beyond the reflection stage and make a positive impact on the lives of poor and helpless people.

I prepared two more short essays on the subject of why rendering such assistance was going to be an integral part of my life:

Appropriate Pragmatism

Many of us overcomplicate our existence on Earth. Since the beginning of time, people have developed complex theories and doctrines concerning how we should spend the limited time we all have during our lives.

Life on Earth should be recognized as simple and straightforward. In my opinion, God undoubtedly intended for our lives to be direct and uncomplicated. Jesus's brief stay here confirms this ideal.

The Ten Commandments are an essential set of principles concerning how people should lead their lives while here on Earth. If we accept Jesus's basic teachings and attempt to practice his examples, we can go much further and live wonderful existences while we are growing and blossoming in our lifetimes. That is because Jesus's teachings and examples are very positive.

Everyone should love one another. The word love has been distorted by many contemporary authors and others. It means essentially caring for other people in the same manner as we care for ourselves. Perhaps the most practical way to love others is to assist or help them in a manner that will make their existence more comfortable and meaningful. At any given time, there are millions of people in the world who are truly needy and in desperate need of help or assistance. It is abundantly easy to come in contact with them. A simple approach is to use the resources of local churches or charitable organizations.

We must never forget who our Creator is, why we exist, and what we are supposed to accomplish during our brief lifetimes. It is fine to attempt to answer these questions and many others through long and detailed analysis of the Bible, church teachings, or simply through independent thought.

The Everlasting and Ubiquitous Truth

Since the advent of civilization, there have been a myriad of different religions. People have worshipped a variety of different supreme beings and gods. Even when the only deity in focus has been the one true God, there was still an abundance of religions in other countries, societies, and cultures.

Notwithstanding the wide disparities in people's methods of worship and religious beliefs, people should never become confused, or disoriented, or improperly stress unimportant concepts. It should never be forgotten that religions are composed of congregations of human beings. Almost all religions develop characteristics and a history to attract a certain segment of the population.

All of the major religions worshipping the one true God exist mainly by virtue of church donations. There is nothing wrong with this fact. It is entirely consistent with the sacred scripture. When this fact is taken to its logical conclusion, however, it soon becomes obvious that the wealthier the religion's members, the more powerful and secure the religion. Again, there is nothing wrong with this state of affairs, it should just be carefully watched and scrutinized.

It should also be understood by members of all religions that the history underlying their particular religion, their distinct church services, and the liturgical messages conveyed to them may be designed at least in part to conform to their personalities, lifestyles, and socioeconomic abilities. There is also nothing improper about these practices as long as they are used for constructive purposes.

What cannot be overlooked and what should never be downplayed, however, is that there are four everlasting and ubiquitous truths that apply to us all, no matter when or where we experience our brief stay on Earth: (1) God created the Earth as a place for human beings to exist for a short time; (2) Jesus showed us by his wonderful example how we should live on Earth during our transitory existence; (3) the Holy Trinity is all-powerful, all good, and eternal; and (4) we should adhere to the Holy Trinity's rules to ensure that we all live good, meaningful lives.

The following queries should naturally spring forth from these spiritual declarations. What are the sacred instructions of which all humans must be aware, either directly through formal worship services or indirectly through natural human impulses?

In other words, how can individuals be assured of living good and meaningful lives?

In my opinion, the answer is to treat all of God's children with kindness, honor, and respect. Moreover, people who take the process one step further and actually assist others who have been largely neglected because of their poverty, age, disability, or other circumstances are to be commended for their good work and intentions.

All this thinking caused me to begin actively searching for volunteer opportunities to assist others. At the outset, I was certain that there would be virtually endless opportunities anywhere in the United States and that Hawaii would be no exception.

I began my search on the Internet, searching for organizations that needed volunteer assistance in Hawaii. Right away I discovered that a meeting was being held to outline the various volunteer activities available to individuals on the Hawaiian Islands. I attended the meeting and planned to determine where it made the most sense to render my assistance. Much to my surprise, however, the meeting was simply a video presentation and was attended by only one individual besides myself, the director of the local health department. We spoke briefly, and he invited me to perform volunteer work at the health department. I accepted and began doing volunteer work there twice a week for over a year.

At the outset, the director and I were unsure in which areas my assistance would be most beneficial. There were fifteen to twenty people employed by the department, so I aided several of them in performing aspects of their individual jobs. Then the director and I determined that the most far-reaching support I could provide would be for me to conduct exhaustive research on the hazards inherent in tobacco smoking. We both thought that if the results of my research made it abundantly clear that smoking was hazardous, then we would communicate this information to the Hawaii Congress and Senate in the hope that these political institutions would take measures in the interests of the public good.

I conducted my research primarily over the Internet. I had my laptop computer linked to a telephone line in one of the office areas within the local health department. I conducted such research twice a week and began preparing documents outlining my findings. One of the many documents I prepared, which is included as Appendix 1, was entitled "Facts and Figures Relating to Tobacco Smoking." After over a year of assiduously performing such research, the director and I met with several state representatives and senators. We presented them with a twelve-page report (see Appendix 2) on the numerous blatant health perils involved in smoking tobacco products. As a result of my research efforts and the meetings we had with state representatives and senators, the Hawaii Legislature overwhelmingly passed a resolution calling for a formal public investigation of the health risks associated with smoking tobacco products (see Appendix 3). The Hawaii state legislature's involvement encouraged local county offices also to become involved, and many Hawaii counties outlawed tobacco smoking in public places like shopping centers, stores, restaurants, and bars.

While doing volunteer work for the health department, I also began providing assistance for other charitable organizations. The Community Clinic was a local medical facility for the island's poor and uninsured. I gave legal and business advice to the clinic director and several of his staff members.

I then began providing volunteer assistance for the nearby Catholic church. Two of the priests there, Father Bill and Father Jim, became very close friends of mine. Father Bill had once assisted the leper colony on Molokai and had provided his services to Mother

Teresa in Calcutta. The assistance I provided to the Catholic church was mostly construction work, although I did provide legal and business advice as well. The construction work was performed over the course of many months and involved the church, the rectory, and the school. My work was somewhat odd to watch. I frequently held onto walls or doorways as I was carrying tools or materials to ensure that I didn't fall or drop items. I also performed as much work as possible sitting down. It usually took considerably more time than it would take an ordinary construction employee, but I always completed the job.

At the same time, I provided legal and business counseling for the Catholic Charities organization, which had specific problems that needed to be addressed quickly. I also became involved in assisting a disabled woman and her family who resided in another part of the island. Her husband was a Japanese citizen, and they planned to sell their home and move back to Japan. I spent many days over several weeks cleaning and making minor improvements to help facilitate the sale of the property.

Next I became involved with the Self-Help Housing Corporation of Hawaii. This program organizes groups of prospective homeowners and gets them personally involved in the building process. This significantly decreases the cost of home ownership. I assisted many such projects with carpentry, electrical, plumbing, and finish work.

At one point, I was contacted by representatives from a medical facility in a small community. I met on many occasions with doctors, nurses, and assorted medical staff to discuss the restructuring of their medical clinic.

At the same time as I was involved in these efforts, I began assisting the regional Salvation Army. Over the next two and a half years I did a great deal of volunteer work there. The Salvation Army assists poor, destitute, and homeless persons, feeding people who cannot afford to pay for or prepare meals for themselves and providing counseling and a variety of different support services. I donated legal and business counseling. I also did quite a bit of construction work, in almost every form of construction trade, on the Salvation Army buildings, including the thrift store, the Salvation Army Meeting Room, the church, and the home of the Salvation Army lieutenants. Additionally, I conducted short seminars on how to obtain employment and how to overcome spousal abuse.

I became acquainted with all the people who were associated with or worked at the Salvation Army. The two managing lieutenants, Kevin and Vidella, are a married couple and became close friends of mine. So did another volunteer named Dan, who was able to help me on construction projects even though he was partially blind. The services I provided to the Salvation Army were so extensive that Kevin sent an article to a local newspaper to summarize some of the efforts I made to improve that charitable facility. Many of the construction improvements involved are depicted in photographs that I took. These photographs are contained at the end of this chapter.

While all this was taking place, the governor of Hawaii was advised of my activities and asked me if I would be willing to be a Hawaii Civil Rights Commissioner. There are five such Commissioners who are responsible for the entire State of Hawaii. These commissioners adjudicate cases involving allegations of civil rights infringements occurring anywhere in the state. They are the highest judicial arm within the executive branch of government in Hawaii. After I served a two-year term, the governor reappointed me for another five years. I felt greatly honored that the governor had heard about and approved of my volunteer efforts. It was extremely pleasing to know also that the highest ranking politician in the state endorsed my belief that it is important to assist deserving individuals.

Another organization that I became involved with is SCORE, which provides free business and legal advice via the Internet. This was very time-consuming work. On average, I fielded about five counseling requests every week from individuals or companies who needed assistance with a wide array of business and legal questions and dilemmas. I have been performing this volunteer activity for quite some time now.

I also assisted a number of local churches. At the Episcopal church, where I was given the title of Junior Warden, I did renovation work in both the church and preschool as well as at the rectory, the meeting room, and the pastor's home. I attended and voted at all the meetings of the management committee overseeing the church. I made very good friends through my work at those facilities. I provided a mixture of legal and construction services to the local Church of Jesus Christ of Latter Day Saints. And at the Methodist church I primarily did construction work in the lounge and meeting area, the preschool, a large unoccupied building near the church, and the pastor's nearby home.

A different local charitable organization that I worked for was the Boys and Girls Club. Their facilities were in desperate need of repair, renovation, and improvement. I performed primarily carpentry and electrical work. Lastly, I helped a women's outreach program that was interested in being apprised of the legal avenues open to them to help prevent spousal abuse.

Although my physical disabilities were obvious, what with my scars, impaired speech, and faulty balance, which people ordinarily became aware of immediately, they generally welcomed my assistance.

It was evident to me that I had begun doing a very substantial amount of volunteer work for many different organizations. I was reminded, in a certain sense, of my pre-accident days, when I had been obsessed with success. However, there was one immense difference. Before the accident, I was obsessed with education, traveling, and my legal career. After the accident, I became obsessed with helping others and assessing my relationship with God. I don't believe my activities before and after the accident can really be compared in terms of what matters in life. Before, I often played a pivotal role in helping large corporations and companies make or retain huge amounts of money. In contrast, my volunteer work improved people's lives. There is no comparison. Comparing my spiritual life before and after the accident leads to the same conclusion. Before the accident I ordinarily spent a total of an hour a week on Sundays in church like other parishioners. The remainder of the week I used my time to plan and complete the work necessary to excel in my job. In stark contrast, after the accident I did volunteer work during most of my waking hours. My endeavors often lasted well into nights and weekends. Perhaps even more striking, since the accident I have spent a good deal of time each day thinking about God. I have felt especially appreciative that God's teachings appear totally consistent with my own thoughts concerning the meaning and purpose of life.

I realize that I may appear zealous, perhaps overly so, in the efforts described above. Despite this, I have been and am now entirely living my life consistent with my motives *and desires.*

Each of the following photographs depicts a feature or improvement that I added to a Salvation Army building.

Photo 1. The front of the Salvation Army Church. The sign at the center shows the times and days of the worship services. I helped install protective siding on the front of the church, replacing wood paneling that was about fifty years old, termite infested, and falling apart.

Photo 2. The side of the Salvation Army Church. A driveway runs alongside the church. I installed the siding and the two air conditioners seen in the photograph. I also ran two electrical circuits for the air conditioners to ensure there was sufficient power for each one separately.

Photo 3. The left front side of the Salvation Army Church. The photograph accentuates the siding placed upon the exterior of the building.

Photo 4. The two entry doors to the church. To the left and right of the doors are two small stands topped by large concrete casts of Santa Claus, which were chained and locked to the exterior wall of the facility. The statues were only displayed during the Christmas season.

Photo 5. The interior of the Salvation Army Church. I installed the covered wall and the electrical plugs and circuits for the devices.

Photo 6. The sign for the Salvation Army Thrift Store.

Photo 7. A walkway I installed to enter the Salvation Army Thrift Store. Anyone using a wheelchair or walker or who had other difficulties was greeted for many years by three crumbling stairs. It was ridiculous to think that for many years the store was largely inaccessible to the people who probably were most in need of the merchandise.

Photo 8. A roof I installed in the right front of the Salvation Army Thrift Store. This roof protects patrons and their children from the rain while they inspect clothing, toys, and other items.

Photo 9. The rear of the Salvation Army Thrift Store. I installed a door in the back wall of the store. A slightly elevated ramp leads up to the door. On the other side of the door, stairs and a railing were installed, leading down to the ground area out behind the store. Previously, there was no indoor access to the back of the store. Customers and their children had to walk out the front door and go around the side of the building in order to get to the back area, where there were many additional items for sale. A large roof was also constructed to cover the entire backyard area and protect patrons and their children when it is raining.

Photo 10. A roof I installed between the Salvation Army Thrift Store and Meeting Room. This is another large roof covering a substantial portion of the outdoor merchandise. Again, it shelters patrons and their children from the rain while they inspect clothing, toys, and other sale items.

Photo 11. View of the roof I constructed along the east side of the Salvation Army Thrift Store, during construction. The wood framing sits on concrete piers; fiberglass sheets were mounted above the framing to repel water.

Photo 12. A view of the same roof from the opposite end of the building.

Photo 13. Interior sections of the double wooden doors I installed inside the Salvation Army Meeting Room.

Photo 14. The outside front of the Salvation Army Meeting Room. The two double doors are visible in this photograph, as is the siding I installed along the outside front of the meeting area and an air conditioner that I installed in one of the front windows. Several people commented that the area now had a professional appearance as compared to its ramshackle nature before these improvements.

Photo 15. Cabinets I mounted in the kitchen located next to the Salvation Army Meeting Room. I also installed cabinets on three of the four walls, a ceiling, a linoleum tile floor, a sink, a microwave oven, a standard-size large oven, a range hood, and two sets of metal shelves. Before this, the kitchen severely lacked functionality. When I was done, many more people could be fed efficiently.

Photo 16. Shelving I installed in the Salvation Army Meeting Room. I also assembled six sets of shelves with sliding doors in this room and installed a ceiling, a tile floor, and three doors.

Photo 17. Another volunteer, Dan, whose sight is severely impaired, helped me perform many of the Salvation Army construction projects.

Photo 18. A storage area that I assembled and installed adjacent to an office in the rear area of the Salvation Army. The storage area measures twelve feet long and eight feet wide. I also installed four sets of metal shelves in the storage area next to the office.

7

Free Will Exercised

A few years after the accident and during the time I was performing a great deal of volunteer work in Maui, three basic facts became obvious to me. First, I really enjoyed helping other people. To be more accurate, I loved to help others and see the benefits of my labors come to completion and be appreciated so quickly. Second, God wants us to assist others, if we are able, which strikes me as a wonderful aspect of the Creator. After my fulfilling experiences assisting others, I felt I would continue doing my volunteer work without regard to whether God espoused it or not, but it remained gratifying to know that God would always want people to help others. And third, I have *free will*. This fact has many ramifications.

The Holy Bible and almost every major world religion acknowledge that mankind was created with a free will. They repeatedly state that all individuals have the option of freely deciding how to act in every situation. While people frequently restrict other individuals from freely deciding in many situations, I believe God does so only in rare circumstances, like when the Creator came to Earth in the form of Jesus Christ and influenced people to act kindly, graciously, and lovingly. The reasons underlying my belief are straightforward. If God were to intervene in an individual's life, then that person's free choice of how to act in the situation would be reduced, if not eliminated. Given the manner in which the world, societies, communities, and families are structured, the decisions concerning how a specific individual acts affect the manner in which many other individuals react, especially over time.

As I've stated before, the thoughts set forth in this book came to me largely independently of any outside influences and often occurred to me during the middle of the night. Once again I woke up in the middle of a night and wrote a document that I believe was divinely inspired:

Free Will

I have not found any clear, direct definition of free will in the Holy Bible. The *Merriam-Webster Dictionary* defines the term as meaning "a voluntary choice or decision." But even a cursory review of the relevant literature makes it absolutely clear that whether human beings have truly free will has been the subject of considerable disagreement among religious and secular scholars over the many centuries since Jesus Christ lived on Earth more than two thousand years ago.

There are two primary schools of thought on this subject: determinism and compatibilism.

Determinists believe that free will is simply an illusion. Every action initially performed by God and then by other human beings integrally affects other actions performed by innumerable additional people. This "billiard ball effect" has existed since the dawn of time.

Compatibilists believe that free will does exist, but not in an oversimplified sense. They agree with the determinists in thinking that prior to any decision made by an individual, there are a host of conditions that make such a decision necessary. In essence, there is always an undeniable chain of events. Nevertheless, such decisions occur in the manner they do because of our beliefs and faith.

In my view, the determinists' analysis fails to be complete. Certainly, all decisions made by human beings are precipitated by a series of prior events. But the summation of these preceding events does not compel the actor to react in a certain, unchangeable manner.

Perhaps the most effective way to analyze this subject is to consider an extreme case. Certainly one of the most evil human beings who ever lived was Adolph Hitler. He may have suffered many harsh and inappropriate injustices before he rose to power in Germany, but such treatment cannot in any way justify the incredibly cruel and inhuman punishment and torture he inflicted on millions of people. Determinists would contend that Hitler's wanton annihilation of millions of people was simply a billiard ball effect, caused by an almost unlimited number of integrally related, preceding events. It is my considered opinion that nothing could be further from the truth. He made the decision to murder millions of people because he was the epitome of all evil within a human being. I largely concur with compatibilists who reason that Hitler acted as he did because of both an underlying chain of events and his overall beliefs. His decisions and actions were a result of his exercising free will. In my view, he made the choices and decisions he did not because of preceding events, but primarily because he was a sadistic slaughterer who inexcusably hated other human beings, especially Jewish people.

In substance, I fundamentally share the compatibilists' theory of free will. Nevertheless, I take the analysis further.

I am certain God has always been completely aware of the influence that an underlying chain of events has on human decision making and the exercise of free will. However, people can ignore and overcome these influences if their convictions and beliefs are strong enough. It is my conviction that God focuses on an individual's exercise of this free will in determining whether to reward that person for their brief existence on Earth.

Since God knows how prior events can influence people, it makes abundant sense that the Almighty would severely limit interaction with humanity. If God were to intervene in response to everyone's prayers, in millions and perhaps billions of instances, the repercussions of those interventions would be almost limitless. The very existence of free will would be limited to a large degree. The billiard ball effect of such intervention would exceed the imagination. The chain of events preceding decisions would be boundless.

Human history also seems to confirm that God has extremely limited interaction with humanity. If God routinely intervened in people's lives on Earth, how could so many millions of God's "chosen people" have been brutalized and murdered in the Second World War? How could so many prayerful and upright people have been slain in both world wars? How could God have permitted any wars between religious people to occur? Why would God ever allow any good, faithful Christians to be subjected to crimes of any nature?

There is another reason that may explain God's limited interaction with humanity or responses to prayers or pleas from faithful followers. Conceivably, God created human beings with free will largely *for their own eternal benefit* after their lives on Earth have ended. While God knows all the repercussions of our actions and is fully aware of how our free will is affected, we cannot say with any accuracy what will be the powers of individuals who have died and ascended to heaven after death. It is plainly possible that after we pass away and begin our eternal angelic existence, we may need to assess *ourselves* and determine how we exercised our free will while we lived. This assessment should be *feasible* for all individuals to perform. Furthermore, it is conceivable that for unknown divine reasons, God may command all human beings to undertake such a process.

Unlike God, humans will not be all-powerful after death. Therefore, by not constantly interacting with human beings on Earth, God is limiting the inconceivable complexity of such countless assessments of free will exercised by all the individuals who have ever lived and are elevated to heaven.

The concept of free will has now been explored, along with God's interaction or lack of interaction with mankind because of human free will. To continue this evaluation, I will now discuss the basis for an inclusive free will and the supposed derivation of that basis.

Completing the Free Will Circle

Paramount in the grand scheme is the manner in which each and every human being exercises their free will, for this determines where they will spend eternity after their lives on Earth have ended. My fervent desire is for countless individuals to realize that in the grand scheme, life here on this planet transpires in the blink of an eye in comparison to our timeless existence.

What each and every person should plainly recognize is that the exercise of free will encompasses a full circle. In my view, all people will be judged on the decisions they made and their conduct in every situation, including conduct that is beneficial, avoidance, self-sacrificing, or destructive.

To begin the formation of the circle, the manner in which people *decided* and then *acted* beneficially needs to be evaluated. Did their conduct benefit themselves as well as others directly or indirectly? Or did their conduct benefit only themselves? Perhaps most importantly, did their conduct benefit themselves and harm others?

To further the formation of the circle, the manner in which people *decided* and then *acted* to avoid damaging situations also needs to be evaluated. Did their avoidance impact them as well as others directly or indirectly? Or did their conduct result in only avoidance for themselves? Perhaps most importantly, did their conduct result in only avoidance for themselves and harm others?

To continue the formation of the circle, the manner in which people *decided* and then *acted* with self-sacrifice must also be evaluated. By its very nature, such conduct is materially different from the first two forms of conduct. It means enabling others to benefit themselves and assisting others in avoiding damaging situations. The individual acting in a self-sacrificing manner neither experiences benefits nor avoids damaging situations themselves.

And finally, to complete the formation of the circle, the manner in which the individual *decided* and then *acted* destructively must be evaluated as well. By its very nature, this conduct is materially different from all of the above forms of conduct. It means injuring others in thought, word, or deed. It means eliminating methods that others can use to avoid damaging situations. The individual acting in a destructive manner neither experiences benefits nor avoids damaging situations themselves.

To more readily understand how conduct fits into the free will circle, let us consider some actual examples of the four types of conduct.

Acting beneficially includes engaging in family life, attending school, reporting to work, and scores of other situations. Individuals can engage in such activities to benefit only themselves or to benefit themselves and others. Individuals can also engage in such activities to benefit themselves while also harming others.

Acting to avoid damaging situations includes not attending improper social events, not consuming illegal drugs, not taking other people's property, and scores of other situations. Individuals can avoid such activities just to ensure they are not damaged themselves or also to positively influence others.

Self-sacrificing acts include performing volunteer work, assisting others upon reasonable request, being charitable or generous to others, and scores of other situations. This form of conduct is performed only to benefit others or to enable others to avoid damaging situations. Ordinarily, self-sacrificing people are not compensated for their efforts.

Destructive acts include arson, unnecessarily violent acts against others, slander, and scores of other situations. This form of conduct is performed only to damage other individuals. Ordinarily, destructive people gain nothing material from their efforts.

The ways in which human beings act in these situations reveal how they use their free will. Is their conduct entirely *good*? Is their conduct entirely *bad*? What normally occurs in most instances is that conduct falls in between these two extremes because of the innumerable circumstances that effect every action.

It is my unqualified belief that God takes all these factors into account in deciding how to reward people eternally.

God also went one step further: Jesus visited Earth as a human being and taught mankind how to exercise free will.

It is especially noteworthy that even though Jesus was certainly capable of doing so, he *did not* grant persons unlimited power on Earth. Even though Jesus was certainly capable of doing so, he *did not* grant persons unlimited physical and mental well-being. Even though Jesus was certainly capable of doing so, he *did not* grant persons unlimited influence over others.

On the contrary, even though he was and is unquestionably divine, Jesus permitted human beings to torture and crucify him. He also permitted an untold number of human beings on Earth to undergo serious economic hardships. He permitted an untold number of human beings on Earth to be ill and suffer. And he permitted an untold number of human beings on Earth to be murdered, oppressed, and treated cruelly by others.

The Holy Bible recounts many occasions when Jesus miraculously cured deformed, disabled, and ill persons. Nevertheless, since Jesus was God in human form when he inhabited the Earth, he was capable of eliminating all deformities, disabilities, and illnesses in the entire world. For that matter, Jesus was capable of making the existence of each and every person eternal and perfect in all respects.

But Jesus did not do so. What possible reason was there for Jesus's lack of action on behalf of all mankind? There is only one possible explanation that makes sense to me. That explanation is that God does not consider human beings worthy of such an elevation. It has been my persistent belief that God will determine whether we are worthy of receiving such treatment only after we have lived our lives on Earth and have exercised our free will in countless situations.

Consistent with these concepts is the notion of how God created mankind. Inasmuch as he is all-powerful, God could have created human beings to be entirely different. Nonetheless, God purposely created human beings in frailty. Presently, humanity is feeble, both physically and mentally. Everyone lives only a few years. We are subject to illness and injury. We are also highly motivated to avoid pain and seek pleasure.

Why did God create human beings as he did? Once again, it is evident to me that God did so in order to give people opportunities to exercise their free will. God's design reveals and gives meaning to the exercise of free will.

The discussion of the free will circle is now complete. Why consideration of the subject of free will is so paramount has also been underscored. I will once again reaffirm my fervent desire that numerous individuals will realize that in the grand scheme, life on Earth is no more than a blink of the eye compared to eternal existence.

I should not continue on with my discourse about free will without recounting some unusual thoughts that I had during the course of several nights concerning the grand scheme. These thoughts, which are contained in the following document, center on the age and infinite nature of the universe or universes.

Universal Consequences

Generally, scientists now believe that the universe is between eleven and twenty billion years old. Physicists typically narrow it down to between thirteen and fifteen billion years.

There is far less certainty about the size of the universe. Its extent is generally thought to be either trillions of light years or infinite.

The situation is inordinately complicated by string theorists, who believe there are parallel universes in addition to our potentially unlimited universe.

It is obvious that some scientists, particularly physicists, are deeply concerned with these topics. Ordinarily, however, the vast majority of individuals are far too busy with their families, careers, and recreational lives to become enmeshed in these exceedingly complex inquiries.

Nonetheless, these subjects have direct theological implications. First and foremost, it is abundantly apparent that to say

God is all-powerful means that God's capabilities far, far exceed human understanding. For God to have created humanity, for God to have created the Earth, and for God to have created an immense and possibly infinite universe billions of years ago staggers human imagination.

God's powers utterly transcend my ability to comprehend them. Despite this fact, God's amazing creations do leave me wondering why, for instance, the universe is at least ten billion years old. And why is the universe either trillions of light years across or infinite in size, with perhaps an unlimited number of planets? Lastly, what possible reason could there be for an unrestricted number of parallel universes?

Pondering these matters led me to a single conclusion over and over again. Given the unbelievable age and perhaps unlimited size of the universe or universes, there *must* have been other episodes, perhaps numerous episodes, of human life on Earth or on other planets in the universe or universes. Furthermore, the age and size of the universe or universes also leads to the unavoidable conclusion that God also created other entities to inhabit planets where their lives could be sustained.

Underlying all this are the ultimate questions: *Why* would God have created numerous episodes of human life on Earth and possibly on other planets? *Why* would God have created other entities, if this is correct, to inhabit this or parallel universes?

However compelling these questions may be, answers can be no more than pure conjecture. Despite the obvious uncertainties involved, I have developed answers based on my common sense. No matter how many human beings or other entities are involved, the grand scheme remains the same.

God created human beings and possibly other entities to lead transitory lives in locations different from heaven. All human beings and other entities, if they exist, possess free will.

If they exercise their free will according to God's imperatives, they will be elevated to eternal life with God. If they do not, they will not.

I believe with certainty that interacting with God is awe-inspiring and exceeds the limits of human imagination on earth. People may wonder how God is able to interact with untold numbers of human beings at once. The answer is simple. It is because God is God.

Unquestionably, the issues related to free will can be an inordinately complex. By comparison, how we should exercise our free will is fundamentally simple to grasp. We should never overlook that our destiny in the grand scheme is entirely predicated on how we exercise our free will during our temporary lives on Earth. It is the tenet of all major Christian religions that after life on Earth, each and every person will be judged by God. "Judgment Day" will focus on whether the individual involved lived their life up to God's standards. If God were to frequently intervene in the lives of individuals, then Judgment Day would no longer have much significance and meaning. Perhaps more important, humanity would really not have free will.

The concept of free will is obscured by the presence of emotions. Emotions directly influence the manner in which we act and behave. They are a dominant feature of our mental existence and are responsible for a vast array of daily experiences. Emotions include, but are not limited to, acceptance, affection, aggression, anger, anxiety, courage, despair, envy, fear, forgiveness, guilt, gratitude, happiness, hostility, hatred, love, sadness, shame, suffering, surprise, and sympathy. Emotions arise in the brain, and their formations are extremely complex. Essentially, emotions are a form of mental computation that occurs with remarkable rapidity in response to certain perceptions.

Given that our conduct can largely be viewed as an emotional reaction to our circumstances, one may ask whether we truly have free will. However, such analysis fails to consider another essential fact: all people have the ability to reason. This, too, is a function of the brain. Reasoning is the mental process of examining the cause or causes for our beliefs, conclusions, actions, and emotions. When we reason, we automatically merge, unite, and combine concepts, experiences, and perceptions. Even though emotions and reasoning are activities that occur within the brain and both are pivotal in human decision making, it seems to me that reason can and often does override emotion. Based on this determination, I conclude that our actions occur substantially as a result of our reasoning. Reasoning may be influenced by prior events, but those events do not compel us to act in a predetermined manner. We choose to act the way we do largely because of our free will. Of course, such conduct plainly occurs when our reasoning processes are driven by strong beliefs and convictions. It seems eminently sensible to me that God would only judge actions that resulted from the exercise of free will. Moreover, it appears reasonable to me that God would also fully consider all the circumstances that in some way affect the exercise of free will.

This is the type of reasoning I did in the months and years following my almost fatal accident. Before that time, I never thought deeply about this subject.

My experience assisting others after the accident also confirmed two basic principles that were even apparent to me in a superficial sense before the accident. The first is that selfishness is wrong and that it forms the justification for countless offenses that people commit against one another. The second, which is largely a converse of the first, is that generosity is a splendid attribute and a superb way to treat others.

During the entire time I was providing support to others, it was obvious to me that I was exercising my free will. I knew that I was not compelled to act in such a way. I chose to do so. They were all actions I decided to make voluntarily.

8

Relocation and Aftermath

While I was in Hawaii performing volunteer work, I had the good fortune to meet Eve. At the very outset, Eve's life complemented mine wonderfully. She was fully aware of the accident and my injuries, some of which obviously remained. They did not make any difference to her. More importantly, she knew all about my unusual new career helping others and fully supported my efforts.

My marriage to Eve was a stark contrast to my prior marriage. When I was hospitalized and slowly recovering from my life-threatening injuries and after I left the hospital and the recovery center, my wife at that time had no interest in returning to a loving, caring relationship with me because, in my opinion, I was no longer a high-profile trial attorney. But Eve didn't care whether I had a highly esteemed social career. What was important to her was that I treated other people in a considerate, caring way. And this, of course, is consistent with my view of life.

One day after I finished performing volunteer work in Hawaii, Eve received a telephone call from Idaho. Her father had been hospitalized with a serious physical infirmity. Over the next few weeks, he remained in the hospital, and doctors identified other serious medical problems. Because it soon became obvious that his medical situation was grave, Eve considered flying back to Idaho to provide him and her other family members with added companionship and support. As Eve and I discussed the situation, it became clear to me that I could also do volunteer work in Idaho for churches and charitable institutions. I knew that innumerable people all over the world needed assistance. And more importantly, Eve could provide support and assistance to her father and family members in their time of great need. So after living in Hawaii for a few years, we decided to move from Hawaii to Idaho. Eve and I both provided substantial emotional support to her father while he was undergoing extensive medical treatment at the Veterans Hospital. Every day for many weeks, I visited him at hospital to keep him company. He really seemed to enjoy my company.

From a moral standpoint, my almost fatal accident changed me materially. Before the accident, I would have been primarily interested in the legal conditions of the area and whether attorneys and business professionals were in high demand. But now I was seriously concerned about the types and location of the people whom I could assist. My guess that there would be abundant volunteer work in Idaho was soon confirmed. I was soon providing assistance to several different organizations in the area surrounding where I resided. These included Genesis, the Life Care Center, the Valley View Retirement Community, the Idaho Legal Aid Office, the Family Advocate Program, a local Christian church, the Veterans Center, and SCORE.

Genesis was a clinic that provided free medical and dental care to the poor and uninsured. Initially, I provided considerable legal counseling to Genesis. I believed they were providing a wonderful service to people in desperate need, but the manner in which they accomplished this had left the organization open to several unwarranted malpractice lawsuits. After reviewing the relevant organizational documents and interviewing the staff, I was able to assess the situation. As a result, we instituted changes that I believe gave Genesis significant legal protection.

The Life Care Center is where Eve's father resided for a period of time after being discharged from the Veterans Hospital. It is a large facility that serves as a home for over a hundred people suffering from severe physical and mental disabilities. During my first few visits to the Life Care Center, I noticed that many residents simply watched television or else remained in bed night and day, staring off into space. Many had only occasional visitors and almost nothing to occupy their time. I decided to entertain the residents by playing cards with them. I purchased several decks of cards and hundreds of chips, and we played card games for fun, betting with the chips. At the beginning of the session, I would give each resident several dozen chips to wager during the games. On most occasions there would be five to ten residents taking part in the entertainment. I also sponsored a facility-wide extravaganza where all the residents could participate in a card-playing festival.

I frequently took residents to the local movie theater. On several occasions, we watched comedies that were so funny they caused many of the residents to laugh hysterically during the movie. From time to time, I also brought DVD movies to the Life Care Center. Lastly, I initiated a public speaking club there as well, similar to the Toastmasters Club. My rationale was that residents would really enjoy an opportunity to get to know one another better and to speak on topics that involved or interested them. I was right. Many residents joined the club and named it the Gifted Gabbers. My activities at the Life Care Center were moving experiences for both the residents and me. During one Gifted Gabbers meeting, I asked them what my visits to the Life Care Center to entertain meant to them. One told me candidly that she was suicidal before she met me. Another said that our group meetings kept her from going crazy. Another stated that our meetings gave him some purpose in life. Several others at the meeting said that on a scale of one to ten, they would rate my visits as a twenty-five or fifty or one hundred.

I made extremely close friends with all the residents that I entertained. Their physical and mental disabilities meant nothing to me. To the contrary, I thought they were all remarkable individuals in that they had to accept permanent, severe infirmities. Unlike the vast majority of people, who only occasionally get sick and can live in their own homes, the Life Care Center residents have harsh physical or mental injuries and live for many *years* in a medical institution. In my view, they should be regularly praised for enduring this continuing extreme hardship.

I provided similar volunteer efforts in the medical wing of the Valley View Retirement Community. The residents of this wing were often in exceedingly poor health, both physically and mentally. I entertained residents there in a variety of ways, such as playing cards and other games. In addition, I helped a number of residents do physical therapy exercises. And I brought DVD movies to watch. My relationships at Valley View were similar in many ways to those I have felt so emotionally uplifted by at the Life Care Center. I became fast friends with several of the residents. I have a great deal of respect for them. They suffer enormous physical and mental problems and largely relate to others in a kind, caring fashion. They, too, are to be praised for their efforts.

In Idaho, I also have spent substantial amounts of time assisting the Legal Aid Office in a wide variety of cases involving civil, criminal, family and governmental law. The clients, who are also extremely varied, generally could not afford the expense of retaining a private attorney, so I and the other attorneys from the Legal Aid Office provided our services for free.

In Idaho, the Family Advocate Program provides legal assistance primarily to women and children who are emotionally and physically abused or battered by fathers, husbands, or boyfriends. The employees and volunteers at this facility also counsel and provide various forms of support for victims. Most of my work at the Family Advocate Program consisted of construction. Once, before I got involved, an electrical contractor gave them a bid for limited electrical work that in my opinion was clearly exorbitant. So I've periodically done electrical work at the Family Advocate Program office at no cost.

The minister at the local Christian church that I attended became a close friend of mine. I performed a variety of legal and construction tasks at the church. The minister also connected me with other charitable institutions that benefited from my assistance. The aid I've provided to the Idaho Veterans Center varied, depending on the facility's needs. It often involved business activities, and even organizational and filing matters. As in Hawaii, I helped SCORE by providing free business and legal advice to people who requested such counseling over the Internet.

Finishing volunteer tasks still makes me feel full of joy, just as it had in Hawaii. I continue to think that I am unmistakably living my life in a manner completely consistent with what I think life is truly about. Hence I continue to do volunteer work in Idaho. I am always open to expanding my assistance activities, depending on my time constraints and the specific needs of the charitable institution.

Much as when I lived in Hawaii, I occasionally wake up in Idaho in the middle of the night with remarkably uncommon reflections that I considered to be divinely inspired. Two of the documents I prepared in Idaho are given below:

Grandiose Portrayal

Atheism is defined as denial of the existence of God. Agnosticism is defined as the belief that the existence of an ultimate reality such as God is unknown and probably unknowable. Implicit in both belief systems is the conviction that all human beings exist on Earth for limited lifetimes for no purpose. Implicit in both belief systems is the basic premise that during life here on this planet, all human beings can be utterly selfish. Implicit in both belief systems is the fundamental notion that human beings exist only to incessantly gratify their desires.

It is my fervent belief that both atheism and agnosticism could not be further from the truth. It is remarkably obvious that all the unbelievably complex but absolutely necessary elements of Earth and the universe had to have been created or willed into existence by some all-powerful entity. Solids, liquids, gases, forces, and dimensions do not suddenly materialize out of nothingness.

What name we attach to this all-powerful entity is immaterial. It can be God. It can be the Creator. It can be a host of different informal and formal titles in a seemingly unlimited number of languages and cultures. It appears undeniable though, that this all-powerful entity created everything. It is my conviction that this carefully considered analysis is irrefutable. Nonetheless, atheism and agnosticism would not exist or have adherents if everyone viewed the existence of God as fundamentally irrefutable.

It makes abundant sense for God to have structured creation so that certain aspects of human existence may be overwhelmingly but not conclusively obvious. God thus leaves it to the individual's *free will* to formulate beliefs. I may suppose that it is indisputably logical to believe that God is the creator of all. The subject, however, far exceeds human understanding. In essence, I am exercising my free will to formulate my faith that God is the creator of all. Many individuals are not willing to exercise their free will in a similar fashion.

Human comprehension is largely a function of human communication. Human intelligence also significantly increases over time as a result of communication. People are able to communicate orally, of course, but the transference of large amounts of information, whether relating to religion, language, history, geography, social structure, government, science, mathematics, and so forth, largely became possible only after we developed the ability to write. Alphabetic writing culminated in the development of books, which are used to amass information and transfer it to successive generations. Humanity has been able to write for a few thousand years. Writing was initially performed on stone and wood fragments and chips. People then developed the ability to write on vellum slightly more than a thousand years ago. Vellum was extremely durable in that it is lamb or calf skin. People began producing books beginning in the seventh century. Books were at first constructed entirely by hand. For almost five hundred years, most books were religious treatises. Only in the thirteenth century did secular books appear. In the mid-fifteenth century, the printing press was developed.

It was difficult, to say the least, for persons in large societies to develop conceptions of the nature of God and the teachings of the Divine Creator before the last few centuries. Obviously, this was because people were largely unable to communicate with one another about these topics except in a very limited verbal manner. It has only been over the last few centuries that societies all over this Earth have been able to assemble sizeable amounts of human thought in books, manuscripts, and treatises about interaction with the Divine. The number and variety of completely different religions is surprising. Millions sincerely believe that the universe was created by a single, specific divine entity, while millions of others believe it was created by a completely different entity or entities.

We must realize that religions were created by mankind. Religions are used to worship a divine entity or entities, but still they were established by human beings. Consequently, religions have been formed as a result of local or regional beliefs, needs, and desires. That there are massive differences in religious beliefs is completely consistent with the concept of free will. Moreover, the fact that there are many different versions of the Holy Bible and the commandments given by God to humanity, which is central to Christian religions, is also consistent with the notion that mankind has a free will. The differences in the versions may also be due to the fact that mankind's ability to write down and thus preserve what was actually said arose many, many centuries after Moses received the commandments from God.

If there was absolute agreement among all individuals concerning the existence of God and the nature of the Creator, then life here on Earth would be outlandishly different. If there was absolute agreement among all individuals concerning the existence and nature of Jesus on Earth, then there would not be disparate religions. If there was absolute agreement that there is only one Holy Bible and one set of commandments from God, then there would be far less reason for individuals to have free will. But there is not absolute, or even majority, agreement on any of these things. I believe that God did not intend for the world to have been created in that uniform way, for if the Creator had, the concepts of sin, temptation, free will, and judgment day would lack any useful meaning.

It is my perception that there remain aspects of humanity's existence that should not be overlooked in determining the meaning and purpose of our lives. Actually, the initial insight has to do with world religions. Even though there may be substantial disagreement as to the existence and nature of the divine entity or entities, there is extensive agreement the world over on one principle: all the major religions of the world urge individuals to treat one another fairly, honestly, and generously.

It is also my perception that there is an inherent desire in each and every human being to be kind, caring, and trusting to one another. In substance, this means helping another person when the need arises. We have the free will to decide either to assist others in such a way or not. It is completely up to us.

The Conceivable Nature of God

God is all-powerful. God is omnipotent. God is supreme. What does this really mean? In actuality, we are not capable of understanding even the most basic aspects of the nature of God, and so throughout history people have largely avoided even making conjectures about it. Instead, people have relied on instances in which God interacted with specific individuals and conveyed specific aspects of divine nature, along with rules concerning how human beings should relate to one another. Many such communications are set forth in the Holy Bible. God also came to Earth for a brief period of time, embodied in the human form of Jesus Christ. Various people added a New Testament to the Bible, integrating the life, teachings, and crucifixion of Jesus on Earth.

To continue and expand its interaction with the Almighty, humanity has formed a host of different religions to worship God. All the valid, major world religions recognize that, with unrestrained power, God willed into being the universe or universes, the galaxy, Earth, and human beings. This leads us, with our limited intellects, to wonder why all this was done. Why did God create a universe composed of a limitless number of planets and infinite in size? Why did God create huge galaxies with forces and dimensions that are inordinately complicated? Why did God create human beings and all life to be so seemingly multifaceted? It has long been stated by various religions and individuals that we are God's children. But this concept alone falls enormously short of answering these questions.

Perhaps the only way to make any progress in this inquiry is to make a logical attempt to view matters from God's perspective. This attempt may be an absurd endeavor bound for failure, but it seems to be the only method we can employ. This logical attempt needs to commence as far back as humans can conceptualize. We know that God has no beginning and no end and is not subject to time. Nevertheless, at some point God determined that its solitary existence was lacking. God determined that its existence was to be shared with other beings. In response to this realization, in my opinion, God created angels. Angels were created with free will. Free will is immensely important for all forms of life. This capacity enabled angels to develop different personalities and characters and allowed them the freedom not to respond automatically in the same manner to each and every idea posed by God.

Nevertheless, imbuing angels with free will had ominous implications, for angels were able to act as they so desired. A group of angels headed by Lucifer rebelled against God, failed, and were cast out of heaven. It is logical to assume that because of the conduct of Lucifer and the other rebellious angels, God wanted to ensure that no similar event would ever occur. I believe that because of such conduct, God determined to create humanity in a separate environment and subject to an entirely different set of rules of existence. It is my view that human beings are primitive, both physically and mentally, compared to angels. Human beings are subject to a host of forces and dimensions that have no effect on angels. Human beings live temporary, transient lives, in contrast to angels, which live forever. Human beings live on a single planet called Earth, while angels exist in the paradise known as heaven.

Furthermore, human beings are all subject to a moral inquiry, for God will take into consideration how each individual acted during his or her entire life here on Earth, coupled with all the influencing factors. It will in all likelihood be a completely exhaustive inquiry. If human beings pass the inquiry, they will be rewarded by God. If they do not pass the inquiry, with the scoring standards set by God and God alone, they will not be rewarded.

Like angels, human beings were also created with free will. Like angels, free will permits people to develop different personalities and characters. As distinct persons, human beings are also able to make unconstrained choices. Given this ability to make free choices, individuals can make decisions that will positively, negatively, or neutrally affect others.

There is a crucial distinction, however, between angels and human beings. Unlike Lucifer and the other fallen angels, human beings can never, never rebel against God in a threatening manner, for human existence is fundamentally so far inferior to angelic existence that it is absolutely impossible.

Existence on Earth, with its multitude of political, economic, and social systems, often leaves individuals feeling disconnected from God. We often become obsessed with our immediate family, employment, interests, and hobbies. Although this is certainly understandable, our reconnection to God is achievable by simple thought. We just need to look, hear, feel, or sense around us to realize that God is to thank for everything. We just need to consider the intricacies of life both near and far from us to realize that God is to thank for everything. We just need to consider the complexities of the entire world to realize that God is to thank for everything.

We should also never forget that God is all-powerful. At the very least, what this means is that God is always with us in some form that we cannot begin to understand. Human beings do have a free will. To avoid destroying this central human capacity, God almost never interacts with human beings. But this does not mean God is not always present with every individual and aware of each action that occurs.

My preparation of these two documents after waking up again in the middle of the night, this time in Idaho, made it patently clear to me that wherever I was in the world, God would still periodically inspire me.

9

The Meaning and Purpose of Existence

During the years since my accident and the performance of many volunteer tasks, a fundamental aspect of life has become obvious to me. As I have told myself again and again and again, I should always try to focus on what truly matters in my life and on what existence means to me in the grand sense. In other words, I told myself to evaluate my actions from the divine perspective: that I am going to exist *eternally* and that my life here is only a *temporary stepping-stone*.

This frame of mind causes me to view events in life in a different way. Many people are fixated on the here and now. They want to better themselves or their situations almost immediately. They want to resolve their problems right away. Often they resist becoming involved with individuals who will slow them down. I, on the other hand, ordinarily reassure myself that events which happen during life here on Earth will quickly pass and should not be assigned undue importance. Consequently, I largely ignore aspects of life that I believe have little or no significance in the grand scheme of eternal existence.

I live such a life here on Earth in thought, word, and most important, in my actions. Occasionally, I reassure others that their physical or mental problems or infirmities will quickly pass by and will be largely meaningless in the grand scheme. Whether they accept my reassurance has varied and depended on the individuals involved.

I once again awoke in the middle of the night and prepared the following document:

Mankind's Ultimate Nature

There are three forms of matter: solid, liquid, and gaseous. These forms include solid objects, water, and air. All three of these forms are found in the human body. Solid forms encapsulate the liquid and gaseous elements found in the body.

The soul is the immaterial essence or actuating cause of human life. It is the spiritual foundation for all human beings on this planet. The soul is not a physical organ or form. Medicine and science have not established the presence of the soul in our bodies or minds. The soul is strictly a function of our belief system, which in turn stems from our religious background and experiences. Though there is no authority on this issue, I believe that when we pass on to the life hereafter, it is our souls or essences that are transferred. God is fully aware of how such a task is accomplished. Human beings are not.

We have no actual understanding of the true nature of heaven. Our limited understanding is based solely upon Jesus's life here on earth, the Holy Bible, and our religious underpinnings. Even still, we can no more than guess as to the nature of the afterlife.

Unfortunately, many people purposely restrict their inquiry on these matters. Because heaven, the soul, and the afterlife are difficult matters to conceive, they simply reject the existence of God, Jesus's life on earth, and the teachings contained in the Bible. Some of these people, like many others, are consumed with the selfish desire to care only for themselves and lead completely egotistical lives. They choose to ignore mankind's ultimate nature.

I believe the choice is simple and straightforward. Do we want to become absorbed by only egocentric, self-absorbed sentiments? Or are we willing to believe and have faith in God and live consistently with the teachings set forth in the Bible, church worship, and charitable associations?

Whether we truly recognize it or not, our existence in the afterlife may completely depend on the lifestyle we choose here on Earth. The decisions we make clearly affect us in the short term. It should never be downplayed, however, that our ethical decisions about the life we live may affect our existence *forever*. It is certainly worthwhile to commit time and energy to thinking this matter through extremely carefully.

People who have already decided to live their lives in a caring, nurturing manner should be praised for their self-sacrifice. Such people, who have not capitalized on all the worldly opportunities provided to them because of their selflessness on Earth, may in all likelihood be rewarded many times over in the afterlife.

One thing has become apparent to me in the years I've spent assisting others: all people were created by God to be truly *equal*. They may have significant differences during their temporary lives, but such present dissimilarities will have literally no impact on the grand scheme of events in eternal existence.

Humanity has chosen to establish different governments, different economies, different societies, different religions, and different layers of social status. In essence, humanity has stressed the differences among people. It is always important to realize, however, that those differences were created and emphasized by mankind, not God.

Moreover, because of the almost unlimited number of circumstances affecting each and every person during their brief life, there are bound to be significant dissimilarities in their lives. Some individuals may be genetically gifted, others may not. Some individuals may be born and raised in a beneficial, supportive environment, others may not. Some individuals may be well off economically, others may not. Some individuals may be destined to achieve significant educational accomplishments, others may not. Some individuals may develop admirable relationships and friendships, others may not. The people who experience these advantageous circumstances often have little or no control over them. Yet mankind takes the results of such circumstances extremely seriously when gauging the level of social status to assign to people.

It is my view that, despite this fact, God will consider such circumstances only when assessing how people have exercised their free will. It should never be forgotten that in God's view, to whom much is given, much is required. This is of vital importance for people to realize. I believe such diversity in circumstances naturally occurs whenever more than one person is involved. I also believe that God is fully aware of this fact and does not feel that the true equality of all human beings is affected by their placement in radically different circumstances.

I again awoke late at night and prepared the following document:

What Existence Is Really About

In very basic terms, people undergo a continual examination of their lives. However, they do not perform the examination themselves. Their lives are the object of God's continuous inquiry. Individuals either pass this inquiry or they do not.

The rules applying to human existence are all determined by God. To make the examination equitable, God somehow had to communicate the rules to all human beings. Furthermore, in all likelihood God inspired such rules in human intuition. In essence, all people *must be equal* if a single set of rules is to be righteous and fair. If a large number of individuals were not essentially equal or were incapable of discerning the difference between right and wrong, a single set of governing rules would be inoperable.

To understand God's rules for humanity, it is crucial to recognize that we are all God's children. This should not be applied in the conventional sense. The relationship is not the same as that of an earthly mother and father with their son or daughter. Instead, it means God created all of humanity. It means that God desires all individuals, regardless of age, race, gender, culture, nationality, physical and mental status, or occupation, to have significant lives. It means that God is opposed to people harming or hurting one another.

God established the world as we know it. God endowed all people with free will. God permitted all of humanity, through the exercise of their free will, to make conjectures about the nature of the divine entity and the rules it applies to mankind. Perhaps even more surprising, but absolutely true in my opinion, is that God permits human beings to modify, distort, or disregard the rules altogether. This is the nature of free will.

God has always been able to plainly reveal the rules of existence that mankind should follow. Nonetheless, God did not do so. In response to this uncertainty and the unsure nature of the Creator, people established various religions and ways in which to worship the Creator. People have even prepared scores of different versions of writings that supposedly preserve statements made by God or Jesus Christ or other deities. It is amazing that documents such as the Holy Bible and the Ten Commandments, which are so basic to Christian religions, should exist in seemingly countless versions, but they do. And it is astonishing how the different religions portray the Creator with diverse attributes and character, but they do.

Yet, a single crucial aspect of all the major world religions stands out. From a *positive* standpoint, such religions teach that individuals should not only worship God, but also treat others with care, honesty, and kindness. These religions commend people who assist others and are generous with their time and resources. Conversely, legitimate world religions make it abundantly clear that people should not harm or hurt others. The Holy Bible and the Ten Commandments may not be limited to versions that are universally accepted, but both documents in all their versions agree that such conduct is ordinarily sinful.

This leads to the ultimate issue that perennially confronts all of humanity: *What is the inquiry to which God is going to subject all people after their earthly demise?*

Given the countless ways in which humanity has changed or distorted the nature and driving force of the Creator, determining which religion to look to for such insight may seem something of a guessing game. However, this would be important if God had ordained only one correct manner of worshiping the Creator.

One aspect of creation emerges as critically important over and over again from every religious vantage point, an aspect that is completely consistent with the notion that we are God's children, completely consistent with the teachings contained in the Holy Bible, and completely consistent with the doctrines of every major world religion: *People should not harm or hurt one another, and they should treat others with compassion and generosity.*

I think these concepts appear to be the very foundation of the rules that will be applied to all people. They can be unnecessarily complicated, but again, that does not change the fact that they appear to be the fundamental rules. It is pleasing to be aware that the Divine Creator's inquiry involving all of mankind will largely involve precepts promoted by every major world religion.

I have spent a great deal of time pondering the subject of whether, stated in its simplest form, life on Earth is simply a test. If we pass the test, as interpreted by God and God alone, will we be elevated to heaven? If not, will we not merit being raised to eternal bliss? It may be that simple. Along these lines, I drafted the following document:

Means to an End

Economics, by definition, involves the production, distribution, and consumption of goods and services. More fundamentally, however, economics involves human beings, who provide their time, abilities, and skills in exchange for money and other forms of remuneration. This is one of the basic activities we engage in during our earthly existence.

Unfortunately, many human beings glamorize the possession of money and all the material objects it can buy for them. Money is often senselessly alluring to them. Many people focus primarily or even exclusively on economic factors during their entire lifetimes. Education becomes a means to obtain the necessary background and credentials that will enable people to obtain employment in a highly salaried field. Too often, the factor of overriding importance in selecting a job is the amount of compensation one will receive. People often attempt to excel in performing their employment activities. Their aspirations in this regard may cause them to work forty, fifty, or sixty hours a week for several decades. When the person retires, they withdraw from their career and relax after working extremely hard for a very lengthy time period. People's proclivity for controlling or dominating others can also be motivated to some extent by economic factors. Communities, cities, provinces, states, nations, and all governmental entities are based to some degree on economic considerations. The same is true of even physical violence and wars.

Despite the far-reaching aspects of economics, it should never be overlooked that it is simply a means to an end. It is my belief that the true end is to live as a good, caring, honest person. People should never overlook or be distracted from the actual reason why they exist on this planet.

There is nothing wrong with getting a good education or a highly compensated employment position. However, it is not necessary for an individual to do so in order to live life consistent with the meaning and purpose of human existence. It is my view that individuals should use substantial portions of their time, energy, and resources to assist, both physically and emotionally, other people.

All individuals should realize that every person's nature and temperament is different for a host of reasons, including their genetic inheritance, their families, their educational and employment backgrounds, the people to whom they are exposed, the mass of situations in which they are involved, and a multitude of additional factors. Nevertheless, each of us confronts innumerable instances where we can live as compassionate persons.

In more emphatic terms: Do we realize that our widely varying natures and experiences are simply a means to an end? Do we clearly understand that the way we conduct ourselves here during our brief lifetimes almost assuredly affects our eternal existence?

10

Life after Death

My life extraordinarily changed after June 30, 1995. The serious injuries from my almost fatal accident certainly played a role. Nonetheless, after I substantially regained cognizance following my long hospitalization, I was a radically different person. My lifestyle was substantially modified.

A much more monumental conversion occurred for me mentally. My thought processes, my overall reasoning, and my belief system were all radically altered for the remainder of my life. My entire comprehension concerning the meaning and purpose of my temporary existence in the world differed dramatically from the way it was before the accident.

I no longer had an interest in advancing in my legal career. Instead, I was wholly engrossed in helping or assisting others in all the ways I could. Following my tragic accident, I lived my life completely consistently with my thoughts about why the Creator put all human beings on this planet.

To avoid any misconceptions, I did not wake up one morning with all these revolutionizing thoughts. They occurred to me over time, often in the middle of the night. I also personally believe that God caused me to think on these subjects and in these ways.

Because it was almost fatal, my accident caused me to strongly and vigorously consider the point to my existence. If I had died, some of my family members, friends, and business associates would have mourned my loss, but they would have carried on with their lives. My absence may have caused some temporary difficulties, but people are extremely adept at adjusting to a change in their environment, even a significant change.

Every aspect of my existence on Earth will end when I am dead. My relations with my family members, my interaction with friends, and my contact with business associates will not continue. For that matter, my learning processes, my interests, my pastimes, and my forms of entertainment will no longer be of any consequence, as I will no longer exist.

Again, my close encounter with death caused me to think about and then analyze what we will experience after life here on Earth. Does death bring our existence to a close in all respects? Are we only able to satisfy a limited number of needs and accomplish a brief number of goals and objectives during the rapidly passing time we have to live on this planet?

Or do we continue to exist in another form after death? When the universe or universes were created by God, did that perfect divine entity intend for mankind to exist eternally for a flawlessly considered reason?

I've continued to think about this topic over the last several years. After extensive mental probing of the subject, a significant review of religious and scientific sources, and noteworthy input from others, I have formulated the following conceptions. The following documents were also prepared at very late hours at night or in the early hours of the morning in Idaho:

Earthly Demise

On various occasions, many human beings wonder whether there will be any form of existence after they have died. Atheists

typically believe that their only opportunity to gratify themselves is while they are alive on this planet. Persons who have
religious beliefs can have a variety of opinions based upon the
type of religion to which they belong, their education, experience, and the persons with whom they associate.

In many of the widely accepted religions of the world, persons traditionally believe in God and the existence of heaven.
Beyond that, conjectures and opinions run rampant.

The brief number of years that Jesus instructed people on
Earth, portions of the Holy Bible, and occasional religious
teaching touch vaguely on the issue of what life after death may
be like. Modern science is also beginning to make inroads into
this query. Physicists often attempt to explain the very fabric of
the cosmos. Included within this fundamental theory are the
concepts of space and time. Involved in this ongoing analysis
are the forces that affect the human race, which consist of gravity, matter, acceleration, light, sound, electricity, and magnetism. Our understanding of physical laws, such as the absolute
nature of space and time, the fluid conception of space-time,
quantum mechanics, general relativity, and parallel universes,
enlarges our actual knowledge of God's power and plan for
mankind's existence. In no uncertain terms, it is incredibly
complicated and complex.

Based on my religious underpinnings and my understanding
of scientific inroads into the subject, I have developed definite
beliefs on the subject of life after death. I believe that there is
clearly life after death and that our soul or substance continues
on after we die. God created humanity, and God clearly has the
ability to perpetuate a person's existence after his or her life
here on Earth. Precisely in what form we will continue to exist
is the subject of considerable speculation.

The following proposition is worth considering. The concepts of space and time play an instrumental role in mankind's

existence in our universe. It is my belief, though, that heaven transcends space and time. God and human beings who are elevated to heaven will not be subject to spatial and temporal processes. The concepts of here and there will no longer be applicable. There will still be a sequence of events, but time as we know it will no longer elapse.

I also believe that the forces which have such a major effect on human existence on Earth will no longer have any effect in heaven. The impact on humanity can hardly be conceived but will include: the absence of gravity, matter, acceleration, light, sound, electricity, and magnetism. Because such a fundamental change will occur, everything we now accept as an inherent aspect of life will be vastly and materially different.

It is my considered opinion that life after death will be so extraordinarily different from any experience mankind has ever encountered, that we will have to be aided by the Holy Trinity just to begin to accept the transition. Those of us who are welcomed to heaven will partake of an angelic existence.

I believe that God is the Creator of all forms of existence in the cosmos. God is all-powerful. God will determine whether we, as human beings, are invited to exist in heaven or not. We will all be judged based upon our short lifetimes. People should never underestimate or fail to consider the obvious, critical importance of our brief lives on this planet.

Existence after Death

God is the center of everything. Every entity that exists in the universe or universes was created by God for a specific purpose. God has reasons for all his actions.

God created man and bestowed upon mankind a free will. It is both logical and sensible to conclude that that the type of actions people undertake while alive will determine where they will spend eternity after life in this world.

The ultimate question that almost all people pose to themselves at some point is whether there will be a life after death and, if so, what it will entail. To develop the best answer possible, maybe we should do the unthinkable and attempt to put ourselves in God's position and determine how to reward truly deserving individuals for eternity. This entire effort is most likely a folly, because God is incomparably superior to humanity. Be that as it may, we must attempt to do so if we are to arrive at any notions whatsoever.

In essence, it may be God's conclusion that only those persons who truly desire to be in heaven are so elevated. The term "truly desire," however, should not be used in its ordinary sense. In God's interpretation, it may mean that only those persons who have lived their entire lives on Earth as good, caring people will truly desire to live eternally in heaven.

Heaven will be paradise in all respects. People who live substantial portions of their lives here on Earth in selfish, injurious ways will feel completely alienated from the all-pervasive goodness in heaven. Consequently, God will not bother to advance them to heavenly status.

God must have planned a meaningful, eternal existence for human beings who are advanced to heaven after life here on Earth. Since God is all-powerful, anything is possible. Modern-day physicists currently speculate that multiple universes exist. Let us also assume that there are an infinite number of planets like Earth located in all those other universes. It is possible that on all those other planets like Earth in the infinite universes, there are cultures remarkably similar to human beings. Therefore, there are an infinite number of other beings similar to humans on those planets in other universes.

The people who are elevated to heaven may be chosen at least in part because they derive joy from assisting and helping others. God plans to reward these individuals for eternity. One way to accomplish this is to permit human beings after they die on Earth to go to these limitless parallel universes and assist the other beings on these planets.

One clear message can be gathered from this exercise, whether it is actually valid or not: God is infinitely powerful. There are boundless possibilities for those who are able to achieve heavenly status. It is up to God to determine how to properly reward those persons.

During my years of thinking on the subject of life after death, I reviewed quite a number of scientific manuscripts. I found physics to be by far the most instructive on the topic. As a result, I developed these thoughts shortly before completing this book:

Forceless and Dimensionless

From the dawn of human existence, mankind has lived on Earth and been subject to a variety of forces, including gravity, mass, energy, speed, light, electricity, and magnetism. The human race has also been subject to several dimensions, consisting of longitude, latitude, altitude, and time.

By necessity, mankind has been required to adapt to these forces and dimensions. By doing so over the centuries of their existence on Earth, people have become intimately acquainted with the means for improving their respective situations.

In order to perform even the most fundamental of tasks while on Earth, mankind has had to understand and conform physically to all the operative forces and dimensions. Rudimentary and simple endeavors like learning how to sit, walk, travel between any two points, utilize fluids, and respond to events in a timely manner are all examples of humanity's need to physically adapt to such phenomena.

As science progresses, it is slowly being ascertained that many of the forces and dimensions are interrelated. At some point in the future, it may be discovered by humanity that there is an absolute unity among all these elements.

It is now widely accepted that the universe came into existence almost instantly after the Big Bang. It is also now commonly accepted that the universe has been in existence for many billions of years.

Even given mankind's complex technology, the universe is still thought to be infinite in size. At least some physicists and even astronomers currently think there may be multiple universes.

Scientific advances are changing fundamental aspects of mankind's physical existence, which will in turn dramatically affect how and when humanity will make physical transitions in the future. It is unquestionably noteworthy, though, that these far-reaching changes will affect our physical, not our spiritual, existences.

Mankind is left to entirely conjecture what life will be like after death. I have formed some definite opinions concerning the nature of the afterlife based upon my close personal encounter with death on June 30, 1995, my perpetual consideration of the subject, my review of scientific books, especially in physics, and my communication with the Almighty. My opinions are as follows:

All persons who are elevated to existence in heaven will proceed to eternal life as spirits or souls. There will no longer be any need for human beings to have physical bodies. These will not exist in heaven.

Mankind is naturally used to the manner in which reality occurs in this universe, but reality will be completely different in heaven. Communication will be entirely different. So will sustenance, rest, and attaining goals and objectives.

To the extent possible, we should be aware that our lives in heaven will be almost diametrically opposite to the manner in which we have existed on Earth. If we attain life in heaven, our reward will be eternal.

My ongoing thoughts on the subject of what humanity might anticipate occurring in the grand scheme of events led me to write the following:

Eternal Life

The fact that God created the world and all life within it is mesmerizing. The fact that God created the entire universe transcends human imagination. The fact that God may have created multiple universes simply staggers all human thought. These actions alone are incomprehensible. Undoubtedly, though, God's complexity exceeds these achievements in an unlimited fashion.

There have been many billions of human beings who have lived on this planet. One thing that is often difficult for individuals to conceive is that God has a personal relationship with each one of us over the entire course of our lifetimes. That is only one single aspect of being infinitely powerful.

Humanity is left in awe and can only wonder why it is that the omnipotent God would have a personal relationship with human beings. Even though humanity cannot begin to understand God's reasoning process, there are logical tenets which do apply.

As a result of mankind's setting forth God's interaction with individuals in the Holy Bible and Jesus's life here on Earth, we know that God is also all-good. Basically, this means that God is the essence of all that is moral and ethical.

Even though God is the Supreme Being, there is one characteristic that we can potentially have in common with the Creator: we can understand and practice decency, generosity, and unselfishness. It is these very aspects of humanity that God has continuously promoted.

God has always interacted with persons on Earth in an abstract fashion. So has the Holy Spirit. Jesus did exist on Earth for a brief period of time, but that was over two thousand years ago.

Belief in God, Jesus, and the Holy Spirit is reduced to only one principle: faith. If a person has faith, it is natural to love and worship the Holy Trinity. If a person does not have faith, then such attributes will not and cannot be present. I have faith. My beliefs concerning my current life and my eternal life completely revolves around that faith.

As a result of my accident and my subsequent consideration of the matter, I believe that it would be senseless for human beings to have physical bodies after their demise. This lack of a bodily presence will mean that individuals no longer have any physical needs. They will no longer age. They will no longer be susceptible to any physical harm. Gender, race, physical appearance, and infirmities will no longer exist.

My conception of the afterlife is complete supposition. To the best of my knowledge, no human being has any basis for understanding what will be involved in eternal life. I have arrived at my rudimentary conclusions based on thoughts and feelings that originated in my mind at the oddest hours.

Individuals will be taught in heaven by the Almighty to be completely moral and ethical. Humanity will be taught to be entirely kind, caring, and generous. Humanity will be taught to love and treat others as they do themselves.

Another aspect of the Almighty's actions that is compelling to consider is divine interaction with others. God decided to create angels. God decided to create humanity. The Holy Trinity determined that it would not remain alone in the endless universe forever.

After formulating the above suppositions, I once again felt the necessity of returning to an assessment of divine ideals. To the extent possible, I contemplated what God may have formulated for mankind to be elevated to heavenly levels. This is set forth in my next essay:

Judgment Day

When God created human beings, he endowed all individuals with a free will. The Creator bestowed on mankind the ability to decide how to act in an almost inexhaustible number of situations.

It is my thinking that God will clearly determine whether or not we are worthy to share heaven with him eternally. Our faith, beliefs, and conduct here on Earth will determine whether we pass this inquiry on Judgment Day.

It is also my intuition that Judgment Day will center primarily on the conviction I set forth in the last chapter: *People should not harm or hurt one another, and they should treat others with compassion and generosity.*

A person should not break one of the rules in order to perform the other. In other words, a person should not harm one individual to enable him or her to be generous with others. An example of this involves theft. A person should not steal from an individual whom they believe does not need all their worldly possessions just so they can give the stolen items to a poor individual whom they believe is in desperate need of the possessions. Furthermore, these rules do not apply only directly but indirectly as well. In other words, a person should not secretly hurt one individual in order to be noticeably compassionate toward others. An example of this involves honoring one's parents. A person should not completely ignore his or her parents in order to have an abundance of time to treat others with compassion.

I believe these simple and straightforward rules completely conform to God's teachings as set forth in the Old Testament, the Ten Commandments, Jesus's teachings set forth in the New Testament, and various church instructions and related books.

In my opinion, God carefully set forth the entire process of Judgment Day. To make Judgment Day a decisive event, God has always been very cautious not to make his existence an indisputable fact. Every individual must have faith and believe in God.

The Old Testament was written by human beings. It attests to God's existence. People are free to believe it or not. Likewise, people are free to base their conduct on the belief that God does or does not exist. It is a matter of their free will.

God brought Jesus into the world to live with humanity for a limited number of years. In essence, the Divine Jesus actually existed on Earth in the form of a human being. As a result of Jesus's life on Earth, the New Testament was written. The New Testament, too, was written by human beings. People are free to believe it or not. Likewise, people are free to base their conduct on the belief that Jesus does or does not exist. It is a matter of their free will.

It is my conclusion that the ability to exercise free will is an integral part of God's creation of mankind. I have no doubt that the manner in which we exercise our free will is going to be decisive on Judgment Day.

Do people exercise their free will to follow God's and Jesus's teachings? Do they follow the Ten Commandments? Do they treat their neighbor as themselves?

Or do people exercise their free will to make decisions primarily to further their own selfish interests? Do their lives revolve completely around only themselves? Are they using their time in this world largely to gratify themselves physically, emotionally, and mentally?

In my opinion, God desired to leave the prospect of eternal existence completely up to mankind. After people have exercised their free will and decided how they will live on Earth in a multitude of situations during their lifetimes, then and only then will Judgment Day proceed.

From the beginning of my inquiries concerning the meaning and purpose of life, I have fixated on one question: Why did God create human beings on *Earth* in such a frail state for extremely transitory time periods? If human beings are truly God's children, then why did we not coexist in *heaven* eternally with God from the outset? My thinking on this matter finally coalesced late one night when I prepared the following text:

Angelic Existence after Death

God created vast numbers of both human beings and angels. Our extraordinarily limited understanding concerning angels stems from a complete lack of any scientific confirmation and only limited religious references. With almost no reliable basis, humanity just assumes that angels reside in a different universe or dimension than human beings and that they exist eternally.

There are several obscure Biblical and religious references to one of the angels named Satan or Lucifer. It is not entirely clear what this presumed angel did to warrant God's disfavor. In certain excerpts from the occasional Biblical account and formal Christian church statements, it is surmised that Satan led a number of angels in heaven to rebel against God. Their ultimate doom is less than absolutely certain. (See Revelations 21:7–10.)

One aspect of Satan's existence that is eminently logical is that God disapproved of Satan's wrongful conduct. Like mankind, angels were apparently created with a free will. Satan used his free will improperly and supposedly attempted to overthrow even the Almighty Creator. That is why the Bible and most of the world's formal religions depict Satan's outcome as wretched.

It is naturally supposed that since God is all-knowing, there was divine foreknowledge of Satan's rebellious attempt, for time exists as a dimension on Earth, and it is universally recognized that God is equally aware of all events that occurred in the past, are occurring in the present, and will occur in the future. In heaven, however, there is no dimension of time. I believe that although time does not exist in heaven, there must still be a sequence of events. Therefore, it is conceivable, but merely conceivable, that God is actually unaware of what will transpire during a future *sequence* of events that occurs in heaven because time does not exist there as a dimension. This is a completely unfounded conjecture on my part, but if this were true, then Satan could have led an unsuccessful rebellion against God without God's foreknowledge.

It is probably much more likely that the Almighty was fully aware of Satan's impending conduct and permitted it to occur for divine reasons that we will never be aware of during our earthly existence or potentially even after death.

It is my belief that God desires not to be involved *again* in a similar series of events with humanity. Therefore, when God created mankind with a free will, the Creator purposely limited such existence to physical bodies on Earth with a multitude of necessities and subject to severely restricting forces and dimensions.

It seems completely coherent to think that following their death on Earth, God will elevate human beings who pass the Day of Judgment inquiry to angelic existence. In other words, humans who proceed to heaven will be created once again, but this time as angels.

11

Recognizing Reality

I realize that my thoughts and many of the ideas set forth in this book are sometimes unusual or unconventional. Therefore, to eliminate any doubt, I will now explain the core of my beliefs. The reader should be aware that I am not simply reiterating formal, established religious positions on these subjects. These are my own independent thoughts, which I believe have largely resulted from God's stimulus.

In fact, there are two major differences between my thoughts and the teachings of long-established religions. First, my ideas focus on the here and now. It has been my experience that all the major world religions, including Christianity, concentrate a great deal on events that occurred long ago. I think it is extremely thought-provoking and beneficial to regularly recount the lives and teachings of Jesus, Moses, Gautama Buddha, Muhammad, and many others who were so fundamental in establishing religions. But the foundation of my thinking concerning the Almighty is that humanity must devote a substantial portion of its time considering the *present* aspects of its relationship with God. How does God desire that I act *today,* in view of all the current circumstances that confront me? Second, my ideas are not limited to time-worn religious doctrines. I go a good deal further. My thoughts are often *progressive.* My thoughts often focus on explanations of God based on human understanding in the twenty-first century. My thoughts often focus on the dilemmas facing people in the twenty-first century and what they can do to live consistently with the Almighty's instructions.

Prior to my accident, I always attempted to discharge my duties as a civil trial attorney with dignity. I always tried to be a loving, caring family member. I also always endeavored to relate to all persons in every situation in which I was involved in a forthright manner. But I was incredibly busy in my work situation. It took a great deal of time to fulfill my responsibilities. I had many cases scheduled to go to trial. Trials could last several days, weeks, or even months, depending on the facts underlying the matters and the allegations. I vigorously represented each and every client, and I demanded complete veracity from them. I rose to high levels at my law firm and in my profession because of my abilities and devotion to the legitimate practice of law. I was highly respected in my field. But in retrospect, I do not believe I was fulfilling my true calling in life. I did not devote the time necessary to the aspects in life that I now think are important. I do not believe I had actually recognized reality, and I was living my life accordingly.

The accident changed everything dramatically for me. I had worked for approximately thirteen years as a civil trial attorney. On that fateful day, the stage was set for my endeavor to discover the true meaning and purpose of my life. As a result of the accident, I was able to engage in volunteer tasks. My performance of these tasks was quite unusual, given my disabilities. Nonetheless, they were openly accepted by the various churches, charities, and governmental institutions to which I offered my services. These efforts on my part not only gave me the ability to assist others in a variety of ways, but more importantly they caused me to analyze what my life was truly about. It became unquestionably apparent to me that my life was not about making a great deal of money. It was unquestionably not about developing prestige and power. It was unquestionably not about improperly controlling other people's lives. Rather, it became abundantly obvious to me that my life was truly about being a kind, caring, and generous person. It was about assisting other individuals truly in need when I was able. It was about eliminating selfish attributes and attempting to lead a largely selfless existence.

My relationship with the Almighty has also become much clearer to me. My endless consideration of the topic has led me to more fully recognize what to accomplish during the remainder of my life. It has also finally enabled me to "realize reality" as I truly believe it exists. Hence I prepared the following document, again at a very unusual time of the night, setting forth more of my conclusions.

Almost Limitless Development of Mankind

During the entire existence of mankind, science has progressed. Another critically important basic premise should be now be emphasized. Science progresses at an exponential, not an arithmetic rate.

What this is tantamount to saying is that in the year 2000, science may be progressing five times faster than it did in the year 1900. This is just an arbitrary example. There is little question, however, that all sciences are now growing incredibly quickly and will accelerate in the future. The same is true of technological advances.

It would be incredibly foolish not to take into account these rapid changes. We do not have to foretell the future, but we should not ignore the obvious. For the sake of brevity, I will discuss just the basics of a few of the more significant and obvious changes.

According to my review of the scientific literature, perhaps some of the most significant changes are about to occur in physics. Consequently, I will address physics first. It is becoming a more accepted premise in physics now that there are multiple universes. This is commonly known as "string theory." We live in just one of several universes. The widely accepted laws of physics apply in our universe, but they may apply only in our universe. The principles of time may also be different or not exist at all in other universes. A few physicists who are on the forefront of these recently emerging concepts are also claiming now that multiple realities exist.

It is not completely clear whether there is any overlap between the concepts of multiple realities and multiple universes. What is definite, however, is that this group of physicists is attempting to establish a fundamental relationship between the theory of general relativity and quantum theory. They are trying to establish a connection between gravity and the speed of light. One far-reaching implication of their concepts is definitely noteworthy. These physicists contend that there are an infinite number of different realities. What is fundamentally important to this concept is that theoretically mankind may have an infinite existence. People may actually never die in a complete sense. Their beings or souls may simply migrate to other realities. The implications are staggering.

It should be obvious that the incredibly rapid changes happening in physics may change our entire existence much more quickly than we realize. We should never disregard the fact that rapid developments in other scientific disciplines may have a similar impact.

It would be a substantial omission not to mention the advancement in computers. In the not too distant future, computers will have awesome capabilities. In fact, in the upcoming years, there are plans to build a completely new type of computer, based on the way energy is radiated. This is the so-called "quantum computer." According to recent technical publications, it is predicted that such computers will be able to solve in seconds problems it would take conventional computers longer than many centuries to resolve.

Medical advances should also not be overlooked. Medical science has reached the level where in the not too distant future it may be possible to clone human beings. The ethical and legal issues aside, mankind has now acquired the skills to make an overwhelming number of physical changes in human beings.

There is one more quality of the human condition, however, that must be mentioned to complete the circle. That is the existence of God. God created human beings and their complete, total environment. God is fully aware of the reasons why mankind inhabits the Earth. Over the last few centuries, scientists had limited knowledge of the fascinatingly intricate and elegant design of the Earth and the universe. As science progresses more rapidly, it is beginning to confirm religious beliefs that the Almighty created everything.

Physics will make further inroads into the understanding of the nature of the divine and all the divine accomplishments. Computer science, medicine, and almost all the other sciences can serve as mechanisms to improve the human condition. As the sciences progress, I believe the human condition everywhere should considerably improve as well.

It is my firm conviction that we should use human advancements to eliminate poverty, economic hardship, and illness. In my opinion, such conduct would meet the ethical standards God has advanced.

The list goes on and on, but we should never ignore or overlook the myriad of possibilities presented to us by the ongoing development of mankind. To do so might be a flagrant rejection of our destiny.

As I was nearing the conclusion of writing this book, it dawned on me that I should highlight certain topics which I thought were of noteworthy significance. Therefore, at another strange hour of the night, I completed the following document:

Conduct on Earth

It is human nature to assume that one's life is of central importance. Many people assume they will have only one chance to fulfill their goals and dreams. Even solidly religious individuals often downplay their beliefs in order to accomplish a variety of tasks that will materially improve their lives here on Earth.

Some people assume that because there are so many poor, sickly, and disadvantaged people in the world, one person can never make any real difference. This belief enables them to simply forget or become totally unconcerned about others' suffering. Others limit their role in eliminating hardships on this planet to giving church donations. Unfortunately, their role is usually extremely minimal and consists of only donating a few dollars to the church collection on Sundays. Ordinarily, they never determine how the donated monies are used and simply assume that the small amount of money they donated is used for the public good. They may be generally supportive of their family members and friends but do nothing more than make their small donations to assist strangers. Even though they often forget what was said during church services, they feel as though their conduct is sufficient to be warrant elevation to heaven, if heaven even exists.

It is my long-contemplated opinion that the majority of people in the United States live in this manner. They spend overwhelming amounts of their time in career, family, and entertainment activities. This was exactly the type of person I was before my accident. I sincerely hope that this is all God expects of us. In fact, it is largely consistent with the Ten Commandments, which focus primarily on not harming others. The New Testament, however, goes even further. It does not absolutely say that we *must* act in a certain manner. It only suggests, by way of the exemplary life Jesus lived here on Earth, that it is marvelous to assist others. Yet Jesus did state the importance of the Golden Rule, which is to love your neighbor as yourself. In my view, such conduct consists of being honest, caring, and generous. This conduct can be directed at family members, friends, or even persons who live a great distance from you.

I do not believe that the Golden Rule means that people *must* provide benefits to others who live in remote places. Nor do I believe that the Golden Rule means that people *must* provide benefits to strangers. But I do believe that the Golden Rule is God's communication to humanity that the Almighty expects all of us to treat other human beings in a kind and considerate way. As stated immediately above, such conduct can be directed at family members, friends, or strangers. It makes no difference.

While I was preparing this book, I continued to contemplate the messages I wished to convey to each reader. Several of those personal messages are contained in the following document:

The State of Being of Mankind

Involvement in a serious, almost fatal accident is not a prerequisite for deciding to alter your perception of life. Nor are injuries to multiple parts of your body, including your brain. Hospitalization for many months and massive medical treatment are likewise unnecessary for determining that you desire to alter your thinking about life. Nor is undergoing intense rehabilitation efforts over the course of many years in an attempt to regain normal body behaviors. In essence, these events led to the awakening of my beliefs concerning reality. These were difficult events that I had to cope with over a long period of time. But no one else has to endure such unfortunate events to alter his or her perception of life.

What is imperative, however, is that people allocate a sufficient amount of time to carefully consider what is truly the meaning and purpose of their lives. People need to meaningfully analyze why they exist. People need to frequently ask themselves what they intend to accomplish during their brief lifetimes. You do not have to be a scholar to study what truly matters in life. You do not have to complete many years of formal education. You do not have to be a biologist or a physicist. Intellectual level and specialties are simply not factors. You just have to make the required effort.

All the serious religions teach that people should treat other individuals with kindness and dignity. All these religions urge people to be caring and unselfish. In substance, these religions have adopted Jesus's statement: "You shall love your neighbor as yourself." This moral duty, the Golden Rule, is found in the scriptures of nearly every religion on the planet. Judaism and Christianity adopted the version of the Golden Rule given above (Leviticus 19.18). In Hindu scripture it is stated: "One should not behave towards others in a way which is disagreeable to oneself. This is the essence of morality. All other activities are due to selfish desire" (Mahabharata, Anusasana Parva 113.8). In Confucian scripture it is proclaimed: "Try your best to treat others as you wish to be treated yourself, and you will find that this is the shortest way to benevolence" (Mencius VII.A.4). These are only isolated passages. The Golden Rule is also advocated by Buddhists, Mormons, Jehovah's Witnesses, the Unity Church, the Unification Church, Jainists, African tribal religious practices, and many other religions.

Human interaction is a fundamental part of life. Individuals are born into families. They are raised by their families and have ongoing relationships with their mothers, fathers, sisters, and brothers. As they mature, they develop friendships and camaraderie. They may also develop companionship with another person with whom they desire to form a family. Then the process repeats itself once again.

There is absolutely no reason why persons should not also establish a personal relationship with God. God created humanity precisely for this reason. Human beings will never understand the extent of God's power while they are alive on Earth. Nevertheless, there is one aspect of God which can be understood and should never be overlooked: God is all *good*.

It simply requires altering your perception of life to understand and believe in the all-pervasive sanctity of God. It simply requires altering your perception of life to understand and believe that God intends for human beings to love and care for one another. It simply requires altering your perception of life to understand that God desires to share eternal life with you after you die.

On another occasion during the middle of the night, I woke up and it dawned on me that I had not yet discussed a topic that can be crucial when people consider why they exist. It makes abundant sense that for such consideration to be meaningful, individuals must examine not only mankind's existence in the past and present but also in the future. Examining the future certainly requires some conjecture; nevertheless it is necessary to do so to ensure the examination is complete.

My thoughts on this topic, contained in the following document, again appeared to be divinely stimulated.

Mankind's Future

Indisputably, mankind's future will have a colossal impact on humanity, both physically and mentally. To enhance the reader's understanding, I will discuss my opinions on the future in terms of decades, centuries, and longer periods of time. I will not set forth the exact number of years that must go by, inasmuch as providing precise dates would be largely conjecture and also unnecessary for this analysis.

Technology progresses at an exponential rate. In other words, science advances much more quickly now than it did a hundred years ago. Such exponential increases will continue to occur.

The physical effects of scientific advances in the future will surpass those of the present and past. Medical science will discover cures for huge numbers of diseases that currently exist. It will also swiftly advance in terms of treatment of injuries. At some time in the distant future, human beings will no longer become ill or be susceptible to physical injuries. Life spans will also increase exponentially.

Moreover, as time progresses, science will make substantial inroads into negating the necessity of consuming liquids and foods as well as the need for sleep. The same will be true of physical exercise. Likewise, at some point in the future, all feelings of physical pleasure will be provided by machines, not by other individuals.

The magnitude of the universe should not be ignored. It may be infinite in size and is certainly comprised of billions or more planets. In the future, human beings will avail themselves of the almost unlimited benefits inherent in visiting and living on other planets. This is another extremely important area in which technology will advance.

Even the most superficial consideration of this last concept leads to obvious conclusions. Throughout history, mankind has been obsessed with acquiring land. Many wars and acts of aggression have been carried out so that one group of people could acquire the land occupied by another group.

On or beneath every area of land are natural resources. A variety of vegetables and fruits can often be grown on the surface of the land. Moreover, wild or domesticated animals survive on the land. Last, but certainly not least, individuals build their homes on plots of land.

It is certainly obvious why ownership of land has been of such importance throughout history. All of this will dramatically change, however, as mankind begins to explore and colonize other planets. As soon as human beings are capable of doing so, they will be able to obtain all these elements and possessions discussed immediately above by settling on other planets. The further advancement of human technology over time will make this effort less complex.

Throughout history, segments of the world's population have waged wars against other segments to acquire land, natural resources, material possessions, or human services. Wars and military aggression have also been carried out to overthrow political systems that are perceived as improperly subjugating groups of people.

The changes that will occur in the future, especially after the colonization of other planets, will eradicate all of the physical reasons why groups of individuals have declared wars on others. Mental perceptions of political conflict that lead to clashes between armed forces will also be removed over time.

Perhaps even more striking will be the elimination of the need for separate countries to exist in the future. Individual countries were established to enable human beings to organize social, political, economic, military, scientific, and educational systems based on geographic proximity and similarities in philosophy, theology, and political beliefs.

Since there will no longer be wars or improper domination, nations will no longer need to exist to protect inhabitants. Inasmuch as living on other planets will become routine, there will be no limit to the amount of land, natural resources, and material possessions that are available. Because machines or other mechanisms will perform every conceivable service for mankind at some point in time, countries will no longer be required to facilitate the social, economic, scientific, and educational advancement of inhabitants.

The establishment of the European Community is a rudimentary example of the dramatic changes that will occur in the future as national boundaries are more and more eliminated. The European Community was established in the late twentieth century to bring about the political and economic unification of Western Europe. This is not to say that human beings will not continue to be organized to advance and prosper together. It will just occur on a much larger scale. Instead of doing so in a national context, people will do so in a world context, to be followed by a far greater context.

Even though nations will no longer exist in the future, the vast majority of people will continue to associate closely with others for a variety of reasons. Political, economic, scientific, educational, and social reasons are the most obvious. Families and marriages will also continue to be necessities.

In the past, families have been required to raise children and teach them the appropriate norms for relating to relatives and friends, participating in school, becoming involved in social events, participating in religion, and so forth. Immediate family relationships are usually loving. Fathers, mothers, brothers, and sisters quite often relate to their children and siblings in a kind, caring, and trusting manner. Many family members relish spending time together. And it is not uncommon for one family member to act in a self-sacrificing way for another. In the future, too, the practice of forming families will continue to be advantageous for all the above reasons. In fact, the formation of families has been recognized almost everywhere on Earth as so beneficial that adoption has been encouraged in most locales.

Another social custom which I believe will continue on into the future is marriage. While the physical pleasures of a marital relationship will be able to be performed by machine, as will procreation, nevertheless there will often be occasions when a man and a woman have romantic feelings for one another, when a man and woman desire to spend their lives together, and when a man and a woman determine that they want to raise a family together.

There will no longer be any need to protect oneself from others after the abandonment of wars and improper domination. There will no longer be any need to be concerned about obtaining land and material possessions, for mankind will have unlimited resources due to the development of technology and settlement on other planets. There will no longer be any need to desire physical pleasures, as all those will be available with the use of machines.

The mental impact of all these physical transformations will be staggering. People will no longer need to be selfish or self-absorbed. People will no longer have to strive to improve only their own situations. People will no longer need to focus only on their own desires. Technology will provide for all the aspects of human life.

When this complete transformation occurs, it is my opinion that all people will recognize equality with others. All people will trust and care for one another. All people will be compassionate and generous toward others, both physically and mentally.

The concept of Judgment Day has had supernatural signifi-cance for all of mankind's existence. It is my belief that Judg-ment Day currently occurs for every individual upon their death. I also believe that once the human physical and mental states advance to the levels described above, mankind's exist-ence on Earth will come to a close and all human beings will exist as angels in heaven.

This last document I prepared summarizes the driving force of this book. I have repeatedly theorized about God's viewpoint on several subjects. I am now going to attempt to set forth God's per-spective in a single, inclusive article.

God's Perspective

We are certain that God exists by virtue of the scores of differ-ent religions, the Holy Bible, common sense, and just looking at the world around us. Crucial fundamental certainties obvi-ously follow: God is all-powerful, God is all-knowing, God is timeless and has no beginning and no end, and God is good.

You may immediately draw the conclusion that mankind will always be incapable of understanding the complexity of God. You may think that it is a ridiculous endeavor even to speculate about God's perspective.

This is undoubtedly true with respect to all the aspects of God but one, the idea that God is good and wishes human beings to act in like manner. To even begin to make progress into understanding this concept, it helps to place yourself in the divine entity's position and make every effort to evaluate events from God's vantage point. This will undoubtedly be an extremely difficult endeavor because of God's unlimited power and timelessness. However, humanity has been offered divine assistance in accomplishing this effort. This assistance includes the life of Jesus Christ on Earth, the Ten Commandments, the

Holy Bible, numerous religious teachings, and the time-honored principle that human beings are all God's children.

Different sections of this book have focused on these individual themes. I am now going to evaluate them in terms of an all-inclusive determinant, namely, the proposition that the Almighty created mankind largely so that each individual could exercise his or her divinely endowed free will in the correct way. In substance, this can be reduced to an absolute principle: *Individuals should exercise their free will not to harm or hurt one another but instead to treat others with compassion and generosity.*

The assistance provided by God to instruct humanity is thought provoking, to say the least. God did not create humanity to be inordinately powerful. God did not create humanity to be inordinately knowledgeable. God did not create humanity to live eternally. Clearly, God had the ability to do so but did not. Yet God did instill in all human beings the capacity to exercise their free will to act honorably and morally.

The life of Jesus Christ totally confirms this idea. As the Almighty, Jesus had the ability to do any of these miraculous feats. But again, Jesus did not. Instead, he focused primarily on teaching people how to exercise their free will ethically.

The Ten Commandments, the Holy Bible, innumerable religious teachings, and the time-honored principle that human beings are all God's children confirm this proposition. Unquestionably, all these sources are centered on this belief.

Religions often go further and declare that persons *must* believe in the one true God, his son Jesus Christ, and the Holy Spirit. But from God's perspective, this is not critically important. Instead, what always strikes me as critically important is that individuals exercise their free will to act appropriately toward others.

For similar reasons, I do not believe that God has determined that there is only one true religion. Religions are founded and often modified by human beings. There are numerous different religions, and they vary, sometimes considerably, depending upon location, history, and the people who practice them. In my view, God regards all the religions of the world that advocate treating individuals in a kind, considerate way as acceptable.

I have stated many times that God considers all circumstances when judging an individual's exercise of free will. Undoubtedly, readers may wonder what the term circumstances means in this context. I will now attempt to describe this term from God's perspective.

I believe at the outset that God clearly recognizes that persons do not have boundless power or knowledge. God is also clearly aware that individuals live only temporary lives on Earth.

More particularly, it seems obvious to me that God recognizes that all people have physical bodies and are subject to illness, injury, and the process of aging. And the Creator recognizes that people are also motivated, sometimes intensely, to seek physical pleasure and avoid physical pain.

God also recognizes that the desires for power over other individuals, for money, and for social status can often determine how people exercise their free will. People can use their reasoning to avoid engaging in improper behavior, but there are frequently improper elements that tempt us to do otherwise.

God also recognizes that at an even more basic level, all people are born and raised in different families, they live in different cities and countries, and they are exposed to the emotions, ideas, and beliefs of many different individuals, exposures that ordinarily influence them substantially.

In my opinion, these are the circumstances God considers when judging the individual's exercise of free will. It is often not easy to treat other individuals in a compassionate, generous way. It is often not easy to avoid harming or hurting other individuals. The reasons underlying our conduct and the resulting way in which we act will all be taken into account by God when he considers the exercise of our free will.

In view of these principles, it appears that evaluating even one person's exercise of their free will during their life will be incredibly complex, let alone that of the billions of people who have existed in this world. It should never be forgotten, though, that God's power enabled the divine entity to create a universe or universes which may be of infinite size and contain billions of planets. If the Creator could do this, God can certainly also judge the life of every individual.

In my continuing efforts to perceive events from God's perspective, another aspect of creation appears rather transparent to me. First, as inconceivable as it may be, we must recognize that God had the ability to create a universe or universes with billions of planets or more. Second, we must recognize that God is eternal in existence and even created this universe ten to twenty billion years ago. Third, we must recognize that God has conveyed to us, through multiple organized religions, that we are his children.

These elements make it apparent to me that God is able to share in the existence of every individual. People are often not aware of this fact because it would undoubtedly affect the exercise of their free will. Nevertheless, I believe that God shares existence with each and every human being, whether inside of them or outside of them or in some other way.

If we attempt to view this concept from God's perspective, we should begin by recognizing that God created every person who has ever existed. It is certainly sensible for God to have done so to share eternity with them. It seems abundantly clear that God deems it necessary to be aware of all the events that occur in a person's life. Undoubtedly, how a person acts is an exercise of their free will and will be considered by God on Judgment Day. Therefore it appears undeniable that in order to judge us and satisfy the interests of the Almighty, we must be accompanied each day, in some manner, by the divine presence.

Finally, one more aspect of God's perspective must be understood. It is crucial for human beings to comprehend God's judgment of mankind and when and under what circumstances a person will be elevated to heaven. We can begin by thinking about the fundamental human practice of permitting others to stay in our homes for long periods. Typically, people do not do this except in limited situations and are careful not to offer this benefit to simply anyone. The individual who obtains such a benefit is ordinarily a relative or close friend. In all situations, this individual must be trusted not to harm others who live in the home. Moreover, it is extremely gratifying if this individual treats others in the home with compassion and generosity.

I have repeatedly emphasized that the Creator is good and that all people are God's children. These statements have special significance for us when we relate them to the question of God's eternal judgment. In essence, God created heaven and dwells there. Consequently, to help facilitate human understanding of Judgment Day and elevation to heaven, it is useful to think of heaven as God's home. God has invited humanity to share his home with him. But this cannot be considered in a vacuum. Like human homeowners, God requires individuals who are elevated to heaven to have lived their lives without substantially harming other human beings. God also requires individuals who are elevated to heaven to have treated other human beings for the most part with compassion and generosity.

It is critical for people to realize that life on Earth proceeds quickly, but we are always subject to God's complete scrutiny. The manner in which we exercise our free will has not only temporary but, much more importantly, eternal ramifications. God has communicated to all of mankind, in some form or another, how to conduct our lives in this world.

In this book, I have set forth many times what I believe are the features of God, the divine inspiration for creating mankind, life after death for human beings, and how life here on Earth should be lived by all humanity. Occasionally, I have gone further and discussed foundational principles that to a large extent have been ignored by humanity. These principles touch upon several topics, such as the following:

• Why people were not simply created in heaven to live eternally.

• The far-reaching impact of free will.

• Why the all-powerful God created human beings to live such transitory, fragile lives.

• The almost logical conclusion, given the incredible age and potentially infinite size of the universe or universes, that there must have been numerous other episodes where human beings and perhaps other entities were created, placed on a planet, and judged by God after their limited lifetimes.

• Why it is that God does not make his presence obvious to mankind.

My thoughts on these and other matters came to me in different locations at different times of my life, but only after my accident. I have no idea why I suddenly began to reflect on these topics. But it is certainly striking that many of these matters were far removed from my ordinary thoughts before June 30, 1995.

Another central thought that came to me after the accident pertains to power. I have stated repeatedly that God is infinitely powerful. Human beings cannot even begin to conceive of that power. The same is true of Jesus Christ, who lived as a man for such a brief period of time. Nevertheless, the manner in which God and Jesus have acted exemplifies a cardinal rule: It does not matter much power an individual exercises, *a person should never use that power to harm or hurt another.* I believe that, setting symbolism aside, neither God nor Jesus ever harmed or hurt any human being, despite the staggering fact that Jesus lived a difficult life here on Earth and was tortured and crucified.

Moreover, the manner in which God and Jesus have acted displays the very opposite of such action. It does not matter how much power an individual exercises, *a person should use that power to treat others with compassion and generosity.* God and Jesus have done this repeatedly in countless and unimaginable ways.

From time to time, it has seemed obvious to me that God was directly communicating with me. This is partially because of the wide variety and unusual nature of many of the subjects I contemplated and also because I cannot help but feel that I should pass these thoughts on to others in the form of a book. These elements repeatedly make it apparent to me that there is divine inspiration in my efforts.

It has been made manifestly clear by God to all humanity that we should love our neighbors as ourselves. A definite way to achieve this purpose is through enthusiastically performing volunteer work to benefit truly needy individuals. There are almost unlimited volunteer activities in every city, town, community, or place where people reside.

Traditionally, the more widely accepted and readily accessible volunteer opportunities are offered through churches. Nonetheless, there are also numerous national volunteer organizations that do not require any formal church affiliation. These include, but are not limited to, the following:

- Activism 2000 Project—Encourages youths to participate in public health, environmental, and educational activities to address local and community problems.

- America's Second Harvest—The largest national hunger-relief organization.

- American Society for the Prevention of Cruelty to Animals

- AmeriCorps—Connected with VISTA, NCCC, and many other national and local groups that focus on community needs and requirements.

- Big Brothers Big Sisters of America—A national youth serving organization with agencies in all fifty states.

- Boys and Girls Club of America—Provides programs and services to promote and enhance the development of competence, usefulness, belonging, and influence of the youth of America.

- CityCares—A national organization with local community involvement to promote local volunteer service efforts.

- Give Five—A campaign that works to raise public awareness about the critical nature volunteer work plays in our communities.

- Habitat for Humanity—Brings volunteers and communities together to build affordable housing.

- Junior Achievement—Teaches young people essential lessons concerning employment and career opportunities.

- Kids Across America—An organization that hosts sports camps for inner city youths.

- Literacy Volunteers of America—A national network of volunteers that administer literacy programs.

- Make a Difference Day—Uses volunteers to aid the homeless, hungry, ill, and illiterate.

- National Exchange Club—Sponsors community services and youth activities.

- National Youth Leadership Council—Helps build caring young people.

- Salvation Army—Ordinarily offers both church and charitable activities. It feeds and assists homeless and unemployed members of the public. The organization usually has a thrift store in each locale to sell items to raise funds to help the needy.

- SCORE, or Counselors to America's Small Business—A nationwide business counseling program that offers small business plan preparation and free business advice services.

- SERVEnet—A portal for information and resources on volunteer opportunities.

- Teens, Crime, and the Community—A national program resulting in teens becoming involved in crime prevention in their communities.

- The National Mentoring Partnership—Endeavors to expand mentoring opportunities for individuals who may benefit from these services.

- Union Rescue Mission—Provides a comprehensive array of emergency and long-term care services, including food, shelter, clothing, medical and dental care, legal assistance, education, counseling, and job training.

- YMCA of America—The largest nonprofit community resource and service center in America. It provides social services to men, women, and children.

- Youth As Resources—A community-based agenda that provides financing for young people to address local social problems.

- Youth Volunteer Corps of America—Fosters and encourages young people to visit lonely and elderly individuals, assist the homeless and disabled, and use their time and efforts to help others.

Conclusion

The reader has just been told about my involvement in a tragic, almost fatal accident that led to a lengthy coma, extensive hospital care, and almost endless rehabilitation and recuperative struggles. All this miraculously caused my life to change dramatically.

After my physical condition improved, I began doing a great deal of volunteer work. I performed these activities at churches, governmental institutions, and charitable organizations. These were places where I was assured my efforts would be directed to the public welfare.

I was involved in almost all these activities long before I decided to write a book. This book primarily conveys my experiences and knowledge gained following the June 30, 1995, accident. These experiences and this knowledge caused me to re-evaluate my life and the purpose of my existence.

I invite the reader not to wait until some life-shattering event occurs before carefully considering why you are here and what should be accomplished during the brief number of years before you die. Unlike me, you do not have to wait for a death-defying accident. You do not have to wait for a dramatic life-altering event such as loss of employment. You do not have to wait for a disastrous event like a death in your family.

I heartily recommend that you strongly analyze whether the pursuits and choices you make during your lifetime are consistent with divine designs and intentions. I encourage you to consider what your actual mission in life is and what life after death means to you. You are invited to give serious thought to how you should live here on Earth and what that will mean to your existence for eternity.

Appendixes

VOLUNTEER TASKS PERFORMED IN HAWAII

Appendix 1

"Facts and Figures Relating to Tobacco Smoking"

Fatalities

1. Approximately, 4,000,000 persons will die on Earth this year from tobacco related illnesses. 11th World Conference on Tobacco or Health, page 1.

2. Approximately 430,000 people will die in the United States alone this year from tobacco related illnesses, State Programs Can Reduce Tobacco Use, National Cancer Policy Board, Institute Of Medicine, page 2. About 1 out of 5 deaths in the United States is attributable to tobacco smoking. State of Hawaii v. Brown & Williamson Tobacco Co. Et Al., page 9. Tobacco alone kills more people in the United States than acquired immunodeficiency syndrome (AIDS), car accidents, alcohol, homicides, illegal drugs, suicides, and fires combined. Food And Drug Administration Et Al., v Brown And William-son Tobacco Corporation, et al., 529 USSC at page 135.

3. In the state of Hawaii, the number of deaths related to tobacco related illnesses in 1995 was 1182 persons. Hawaii Department

of Health, Tobacco Prevention and Education Project, page 1. It is now 6 years later and the mortality rate has undoubtedly increased.

Illnesses

1. Smoking tobacco products causes many, many serious health problems including: cancer, coronary artery disease, chronic bronchitis, artherosclerotic peripheral vascular disease, chronic obstructive pulmonary disease, intrauterine growth retardation, emphysema, heart disease, lung disease, harmful effects on the brain and nervous system chemistry, and significant health effects on unborn fetuses and newborn children. Food And Drug Administration v. Brown And Williamson Tobacco Corporation, et al., 529 USSC at page 137; Oncology Vol. 13, No. 12 (December 1999). Smoking tobacco products causes many additional health problems. They are not all mentioned here to keep this document reasonably brief.

Nicotine

1. There are over 60,000 studies documenting the presence of nicotine in tobacco products, Tobacco Industry Misconduct, What They Did And Did Not Do, page 3. As early as 1972, one Philip Morris researcher stated Without nicotine there would be no smoking …" Id at 3.

2. More than 90 percent of smokers are hooked before they reach the age of 21 and less than 1.5 percent quit while they are teens. Tobacco: The Moral Issues, Joseph A. Califano, Jr., page 1.

3. <u>In 1988, the American Cancer Society reported that tobacco addiction caused by nicotine is at a level similar to heroin and cocaine addiction</u>. American Cancer Society-Cancer Facts and Figures 1998: Tobacco Use, page 3.

4. <u>Two-thirds of adults who smoke say they wish they could quit. Seventeen million try to quit each year but less than 10 percent succeed. Three out of four adults say they are addicted to smoking, although by many notable estimates that number is higher</u>. Statement on Nicotine Containing Cigarettes, David Kessler, M.D.

5. <u>Shockingly, despite the longstanding evidence on this issue, the, FDA was informed that cigarette companies were genetically manipulating nicotine levels so that the average amount of nicotine was not 2.5 to 3.0 percent as was ordinary but instead was 8.0 percent</u>. **A** Question Of Intent, David Kessler, page 186.

Economics

1. <u>In the United States, the direct economic costs associated with tobacco smoking will be 50 billion dollars annually</u>. Short Term Economic and Health Benefits of Smoking Cessation, page 2. <u>Another 50 billion in costs will be incurred for indirect expenses related to smoking which include morbidity and mortality rates</u>. Id at 2.

2. <u>In Hawaii, the direct economic costs include: ambulatory, hospital, nursing home, drug and other expenses. In 1993, almost 10 years ago, those costs, only direct not indirect costs, totaled over $173,000,000.</u> Centers for Disease Control (CDC).

3. In 1995, the Hawaii Department of Health set forth in an article authored by its staff that the total economic expenses of smoking, related illnesses and deaths, both the direct and indirect costs, were approximately $328,231,000. If we factor in an extremely low inflation rate of 3 percent then the current annual cost of smoking related injuries and deaths are $387,312,580.

4. In striking contrast, both the federal and state governments make only about $35,000,000 from taxing cigarette and tobacco products sales in Hawaii. CDC's Tobacco Info-State & National Tobacco Control Highlights-Hawaii.

Dr. Lorrin Pang   Roger Rizzo

Appendix 2

Presentation to the Hawaii State Legislature

—*By Roger Daniel Rizzo*

Joseph A. Califano, the former Secretary of the Federal Health, Education and Welfare Department and the current President of the National Center on Addiction and Substance Abuse, stated, and I will quote him,

"Cigarettes are the only product sold in America that,
when used as intended,
kill and maim millions of individuals who use them."

Michael Pertschuk, the former Chairman of the Federal Trade Commission and Chief Counsel to the United States Senate Commerce Committee, was as candid. He made the unforgettable point that there are 50 million cigarette addicts in this country. He also said and I will quote him as well,

"So even if the companies lacked
the kind of political and economic power they have,
it's not likely we would do what we should do, or what a civi-
lized society would do,
if cigarettes were a proposed new product, which is
put anybody in jail who sold it."

Ladies and gentlemen of the legislature, Dr. Pang has given you information about the medical and health aspects of people smoking tobacco products. I am going to focus on the legal and business aspects of the same topic. Unlike Dr. Pang, I am not an employee of the Maui Health Department. I am a former civil trial attorney in one of the largest law firms in the United States. I successfully tried many huge cases all over this country. Typically, I represented defendants in litigation. My specialty towards the end of my career was toxic tort law. That means I represented large corporations, which were at least accused by individuals, of exposing them to supposed toxic or deleterious substances, like electromagnetic fields, (the EMF controversy), certain chemical wastes, or fire and explosive products.

At first glance, it may appear to some of you that I was on the wrong side of litigation. Some of you may think that to some extent, I sold myself out to the big corporations. But in reality, I always insisted on complete honesty from my clients and the plaintiffs. As a result, if my client in a particular case caused clear harm to the plaintiffs or their families, then we would compensate the plaintiffs a great deal for the hardships they endured. Conversely, if the plaintiffs were fabricating their claims or my client's involvement with their dilemma, which happened a lot more often then you might expect, I fully litigated the case so that what really transpired would come to light. Again, honesty has always been my number one priority.

About six years ago, I was in an almost fatal motor vehicle accident. I suffered many injuries and was in two different hospitals for over six months. Because of my speaking impairment, I have not been able to return to work as a trial attorney since the date of my accident.

I am here today in front of you for a single reason. It is from a sense of shock and shame to be a part of the human community which allows the sales of tobacco products that cause widespread, wanton death and disease. This is permitted so that cigarette and tobacco producing companies can and do make a huge amount of money. This is the entire dilemma upon which we can and should focus.

For centuries, the government in this country has heartily endorsed tobacco products sales for two reasons. First, government officials were never fully advised by cigarette and/or tobacco producing companies of the numerous and very serious health hazards caused by the smoking of tobacco products. Second, the cigarette and/or tobacco products industry is a multi-billion dollar industry, a huge industry in this country. Very few public officials have ever had the nerve and determination to take on the tobacco products industry. On this latter subject, one tobacco products industry executive had the audacity to say, and I am quoting him verbatim, ***"We have more money than God!"***

This statement is a clear slap in the face to all of us. It demonstrates the unlimited power tobacco companies, at least think they have in this country. But, like Dr. Pang, I am asking you, no I am pleading with you, let us not let tobacco products companies exercise complete unrestrained power against the residents of the State of Hawaii. Let us not permit these companies to cause the deaths and infirmities of many, many persons who live in this beautiful state so that tobacco company executives can further line their pockets with money they have made resulting in the deaths and illnesses of many of the residents in this state.

At this juncture, I am going to shift and make some legal observations. There is no better place to start than with a very recent and completely relevant United States Supreme Court case.

On March 21, 2000, which was a very short time ago in the legal world, the United States Supreme Court decided the Food and Drug Administration, et al. v Brown & Williamson Tobacco Corporation, et al. case. The United States Supreme Court is the highest court in our land. Its legal decisions cannot be appealed because there is no higher court in America which can overturn U.S. Supreme Court decisions.

The U.S. Supreme Court decided the Food and Drug Administration case by the tiniest of margins against the FDA. The defendants in the case, the parties being sued, were a large group of tobacco manufacturers, retailers, and advertisers. They initially filed a lawsuit against the FDA in Federal Court in North Carolina, a state where tobacco products production plays a huge part in the state economy. The respective parties lost and won different portions of the court waged battle, until the final legal appeal was brought before the United States Supreme Court.

Initially, the U.S. Supreme Court observed that the FDA issued a final rule entitled **"Regulations Restricting the Sale and Distribution of Cigarette and Smokeless Tobacco to Protect Children and Adolescents."** Food and Drug Administration et al v Brown & Williamson Tobacco Corporation et al., 146 L. Ed 2nd page 130. The Supreme Court took note of the fact that the FDA determined **"nicotine is a drug and that cigarettes and smokeless tobacco are drug delivery devices"** ID at 130. The Court went on to observe that the FDA found **"Specifically, nicotine** exerts psychoactive, or mood altering effects on the brain that cause and sustain addiction," Id at 130. The FDA clearly set forth that tobacco products are highly addictive because they contain specific amounts of nicotine. According to the United States Supreme Court, the FDA concluded that **"the only way to reduce the amount of tobacco-related illness and mortality was to reduce the level of addiction,"** ID at 130.

On the same very important subject, David Kessler, M.D., then the FDA department head, stated concisely in a 1994 article entitled: <u>Statement on Nicotine-Containing Cigarettes, the following facts</u>:

1. **Two-thirds of adults who smoke say they wish they could quit.**

2. **Seventeen million try to quit each year, but fewer than on out of ten succeed. For every smoker who quits, nine try and fail.**

3. **Three out of four adult smokers say they are addicted. Buy some estimates, as many as seventy-four to ninety percent are addicted.**

4. **Eight out of ten smokers say they wish they had never started smoking.**

David Kessler went on to write a book very recently, entitled *A Question of Intent* in which he quotes one cigarette company executive as saying,

> *"Current research is directed toward increasing the nicotine levels ..."*

Id at 167. On page 186 of the book, it was confirmed by a cigarette company employee who informed the FDA that cigarette companies were genetically manipulating nicotine levels so that the average amount of nicotine in cigarettes was not 2.5 to 3.0 percent, as was ordinary, but instead was 8.0 percent. In this book, it was also stated by one very high level cigarette company executive that:

"We (meaning cigarette company executives) all know that it (meaning a cigarette) is addictive."
Id at 172.

It is difficult to believe that this has been public knowledge for a long time, but we cannot ignore the fact the U. S. Surgeon General reported in 1988, in a public report, that *tobacco addiction is at a level similar to heroin and cocaine addiction.* American Cancer Society-Cancer Facts and Figures 1998: Tobacco Use, page 3.

In returning to our legal discussion though, it is critically important for us to take note of the U.S. Supreme Court's observations on page 135 of the Food and Drug Administration opinion. On that page, the Court states that:

"In its rulemaking proceeding, the FDA quite exhaustively documented that tobacco products are unsafe, dangerous, and cause great pain and suffering from illness. It found that tobacco use is the single leading cause of preventable death in the United States"

It went on to state that:

"More than 400,000 people die each year from tobacco related illnesses such as cancer, respiratory illnesses, and heart disease, often suffering long and painful deaths and that tobacco alone

kills more people each year in the United States than immuno-deficiency syndrome (AIDS), car accidents, alcohol, homicides, illegal drugs, suicides and fires combined"
Id at page 135.

Unbelievably, 500 million worldwide will eventually be killed by tobacco. The 11th World Conference on Tobacco or Health, states, on page 1,

"Approximately 4,000,000 people globally will die from tobacco related illnesses this year alone. By the year 2030, 10,000,000 people will die each year. Currently, smoking deaths are responsible for 1 out of 10 deaths on earth."

Extremely unfortunately, the Supreme Court in the United States ultimately decided that over the last thirty-five years, the U.S. Congress has acted consistently and in such a manner which makes it clear that:

The Federal Food and Drug Administration lacks the authority to regulate tobacco products, Id at 148.

The Court went on to observe that the United States Congress, not a federal agency, has the power to regulate tobacco products and in accordance with that power Congress enacted several statutes creating a regulatory scheme for cigarettes and smokeless tobacco.

In simple terms, what the highest court in our land recently held was that the jurisdiction to at least initially regulate cigarettes and tobacco products should lie with the legislative branch, not some government department or agency. This is exactly why we are here and appearing in front of you today.

Both the federal and state legislatures tax cigarettes and tobacco products. Oncology Vol. 13, No 12, (December 1999), page 3 Forty-two states have laws restricting smoking tobacco products at government work sites and twenty states have laws restricting smoking at private work sites. Id at Page 2. Unfortunately, the State of Hawaii has no restrictions on smoking in private work sites. CDC's Tobacco Info-State and National Tobacco Control Highlights-Hawaii, at page 3. Smoking tobacco in parts of all restaurants is also permitted in Hawaii. Id.

Perhaps, the most troubling aspect concerning Hawaii legislators is that they have looked the other way historically when tobacco was involved. For example, in 1996, five years ago, 59,810 Hawaiian youths were exposed to second-hand tobacco smoke in their very own homes. Id.

In Hawaii, surprisingly, cigarette and tobacco product use is only extremely, narrowly regulated. Hawaii Revised Statutes, Chapter 328. In Hawaii, in a nutshell, tobacco products are not permitted to be sold to minors, smoking or tobacco ingestion is not permitted in state government worksites, and cigarette sales from vending machines is prohibited in areas where minors have access. Id. Tobacco companies also settled recently with many states, including Hawaii, and are required to reimburse the settling states in a extremely limited way for the widespread illnesses and diseases caused by peoples' widespread use and addiction to tobacco products.

The settlement referred to in the preceding paragraph appears on paper to involve a large amount of money, but you need to view the entire issue. Tobacco companies have taken the lives of millions of people. They have made even more people sick and debilitated. On the surface, the tobacco settlement may seem to involve a substantial amount of money but it is in reality, only a pittance of the costs federal and state governments incur. Tobacco products companies are still making money hand over fist and causing the deaths and illnesses, of many Americans, and of particular importance Hawaiian citizens, every single day.

The Hawaii Food, Drug, and Cosmetic Act is contained in Hawaii Revised Statute Chapter 328. All of the state's powers to deal with foods drugs and cosmetics are set forth in the Act. For some unknown reason or reasons, in the definitions section of the statute, Chapter 328-1 it is specifically stated that:

"The term (referring to a Consumer Commodity) shall not include: (2) Any tobacco or tobacco products".

In essence, this means that the Hawaii legislature determined, in the past, for unexplained reasons, that tobacco products would not be regulated in the State of Hawaii.

This is unbelievably striking. Given the unquestionable lethal and otherwise extremely harmful effects of smoking tobacco products, the Hawaii legislature decided purposely to side-step the issue. Attaching the most favorable interpretation to the Hawaii legislature's conduct, maybe legislators in this state thought they would leave it up to federal agencies and departments to regulate tobacco use by U.S. citizens. *Unfortunately,* the FDA case decided just a short time ago by the U.S. Supreme Court removes any power from the federal department best suited to regulate tobacco products use, the FDA, essentially tying their hands. *Now* that duty is imposed, in all notable respects, on federal and state legislatures.

But before we address our specific legislative request, we would be incredibly remiss if we did not discuss specific economic issues. Cigarette production is an incredible cash cow. Warren Buffet, who owns ABC television, among other things, implied that cigarettes are the *most profitable product ever conceived.*

Tobacco products incredible profits depend on access to children and its addictive nature. Tobacco, The Moral Issues, Joseph A. Califano (1998) at page 1. Tobacco executives and their hired guns, lawyers, sing the same chorus:

> *"We don't want children to smoke, but that is their parents'*
> *responsibility, not ours."*
> Id at **2**.

Unfortunately, more than 90 percent of smokers are hooked before they reach twenty-one years of age and less than 1.5 percent of teen smokers quit while they are teens. Id at 1.

Tobacco use drains the U.S. economy of more than 100 billion in health care costs and lost productivity. Forty-three percent of the costs are paid for by government sources, including Medicaid and Medicare. The fact that the economic costs caused by people in this country smoking tobacco, after adjusting for inflation, exceed $100 billion a year does not even include the costs associated with diseases caused by environmental tobacco smoke, burn care resulting from cigarette smoking-related fires, or prenatal care for low-birth weight infants of mothers who smoke. American Cancer Society-Cancer Facts and Figures 1998: Tobacco Use, pages 2 and 3.

More directly for our purposes, every year the State of Hawaii receives approximately $35,000,000 dollars because of the state taxation of cigarettes, cigars and tobacco products. CDC's Tobacco Info-State & National Tobacco Control Highlights-Hawaii. At first glance, this appears to be a great deal of money. But the other side of the equation, the costs which are incurred because of tobacco products use, must also be examined and they are overwhelming. The State of Hawaii incurs a huge expense in medically caring for residents and tourists alike here who are suffering from tobacco product related illnesses and diseases. Furthermore, we cannot nor should we ignore that a multitude of residents of the State of Hawaii die every year from smoking tobacco products and it costs a substantial amount of money to residents in our state for lost productivity and for funeral expenses.

Specifically, in 1993, almost 10 years ago, the following medical costs in this state were all related to smoking:

Ambulatory	$48,080,000
Hospital	52,040,000
Nursing Home	33,660,000
Drugs	10,920,000
Other	29,270,000
Total	**$173,970,000**

What is incredibly noteworthy from an economic standpoint in this state is that smoking cigarettes and tobacco products caused Hawaii residents about five times as much in medical care than the state receives in taxable income from tobacco sales. These figures also do not take into account sick leaves, loss of productivity or funeral costs caused by tobacco products smoking.

Lastly, there is another factor which should be examined to get the complete, economic picture. Ladies and gentlemen of the legislature, you may already know this, but I do not want to be incomplete by skipping over it. It would be senseless to ignore any hands raised in the State of Hawaii due to tobacco agriculture and tobacco manufacturing. However, no tobacco is grown and there are no tobacco products manufacturing plants here in Hawaii. CDC's State: Tobacco Behavior, Economics & Health Cost. So the answer to both questions above is a resounding "NO."

Economically, (1) Hawaii derives no income from the growth of tobacco or the manufacturing of tobacco products and (2) much more than five times is spent by the State of Hawaii and its residents for health care and related costs caused by smoking tobacco products than is raised in taxation of those products by the state. The answer then is simple from an economic standpoint alone, tobacco products, especially cigarettes, is a massive losing proposition monetarily in the State of Hawaii without even considering the widespread death and physical infirmities it causes.

Therefore, with everything that Dr. Pang and I have brought up, we hereby are making the following legislative requests. We ask this legislature to repeal Chapter 328-1 subsection (2) which excludes: **"Any tobacco or tobacco products;"** from the jurisdiction of the Hawaii Food, Drug and Cosmetic Act. This Legislature has already repealed all of Section 328-2.1, so another repeal in the same section is not an unwarranted request.

Then we would request that this legislature ban all tobacco related products from being sold to Hawaii residents, not tourists from other states who are vacationing or visiting here in Hawaii. By creating this exception for tourists, or in other words not Hawaii residents, we believe that this state would not suffer any real loss of revenue in terms of tourism as a result of this endeavor and many Hawaii residents' lives would be spared and far fewer residents here, in this beautiful State of Hawaii, would be subjected to a variety of serious illnesses and economic catastrophes.

Presentation to the Hawaii State Legislature, by Roger Daniel Rizzo, continued:

We understand that there are reasons why this legislature, at least initially, would prefer to regulate tobacco and cigarette smoking as opposed to banning it outright Although we do not agree wholeheartedly with this approach, we believe it would be much preferable to the existing situation and have the following suggestions to offer concerning a tobacco products regulatory scheme.

We strongly believe that Hawaii State Tobacco Regulations should, at the very least, cover the following areas:

1. Statutorily imposed modifications to the ingredients or makeup of cigarettes and other tobacco products. After all the impartial, accurate scientific research was completed over the last few years, it is now abundantly obvious that tobacco products are both highly addictive and contain many substances which cause injury and death to individuals smoking such products. Therefore, from a scientific, rational, and moral standpoint we believe it is imperative to require tobacco products manufacturers to make the following changes to their

products before permitting the products to be imported into the State of Hawaii.

a. It is now clear that nicotine is as addictive as heroin or cocaine. <u>American Cancer Society-Cancer Facts and Figures 1998</u>: (Tobacco Use, page 3). Cigarette and tobacco products manufacturers should be required to remove all nicotine from their products before such products are permitted into the State of Hawaii.

b. It is well documented that cigarettes and tobacco products contain dozens of carcinogens. <u>Signal Transduction and Cancer Research</u> (Kleinsmith, page 1) Smokers develop cancer and die in astoundingly huge numbers. Let us bring an end to this in the State of Hawaii. Tobacco manufacturers should be required to remove every carcinogen from tobacco products before those products are permitted into this state.

c. Even the United States Supreme Court recognized approximately a year and a half ago that more than 400,000 people die each year, in this country alone, from tobacco-related illnesses such as cancer, respiratory illnesses, and heart disease, often suffering long and painful deaths, and that tobacco alone kills more people each year in the United States than acquired immunodeficiency syndrome (AIDS), car accidents, alcohol, homicides, illegal drugs, suicides, and fires combined! Food and Drug Administration et al. v Brown & Williamson Tobacco Corporation et al., 146 L. Ed 2nd pages 121, 135.

Unfortunately, in our opinion, the Supreme Court was not willing to stand up for the peoples' rights in this country. We plead with you, ladies and gentlemen of this legislature, to show the courage and resolve to stand up for the rights of the residents of this state and require cigarette and tobacco products manufacturers to remove all substances contained in their products which have been proven to have a harmful effect on human physiology. In other words, the import of such products should not be permitted into the State of Hawaii unless tobacco products manufacturers have convinced the Hawaii State Health Department that they have removed all of the harmful ingredients from their products, contained in cigarettes and tobacco products.

2. <u>Tobacco Excise Taxes</u>: These state imposed taxes should be increased dramatically. This will have two different notable effects. As we stated before, the State of Hawaii receives approximately $35,000,000 a year from the taxation of tobacco products. Unfortunately, the medical costs incurred by residents of this state related to smoking exceed $173,000,000. This also does not take into account sick leaves, loss of productivity and funeral costs caused by tobacco products smoking. So the first effect is that the state through raising tobacco product taxes will be able to recoup more of the extensive funds spent annually to pay for tobacco usage problems.

    Another equally important factor is that the cost of smoking tobacco products has a clear effect on both adult and teenage smokers. Tobacco Control-Lantz, et al., pages 14-16. The extent to which higher tobacco products taxation will diminish the use of such products is categorically related to the increase in the price of tobacco products. Id at 14. In fact, several scientific studies suggest that teenagers may be more responsive than adults to increases in cigarette prices. Id.

3. <u>Tobacco Advertising Restrictions</u>: Of all consumer products, cigarettes are the most heavily advertised and marketed. Tobacco Control-Lantz, et al., page 10. There is overwhelming concern from several sources that tobacco advertising and marketing, including the distribution of promotional products such as clothing, sporting equipment, and gear for outdoor activities, is strongly associated with youth smoking. Id. In slightly different terms, it is well documented that youth awareness of tobacco marketing campaigns, receipt of free tobacco samples, and acceptance of tobacco company direct mail promotional paraphernalia are directly related to susceptibility to tobacco use. Id.

Complete bans on tobacco advertising in scientific studies have led to the inescapable conclusion that tobacco consumption decreased by 6 percent. Id. This may seem to be only a nominal result but, in reality could be a really important effect publicly, when viewed in the entirety of the situation.

4. <u>School-Based Educational Interventions</u>: A large number of school-based programs advocating reduction in tobacco products use have been implemented in schools across the country in the past three decades. Tobacco Control-Lantz, et al., page 3. Most of these efforts have targeted elementary or middle school students. Id. Such programs need to be implemented all the way up to and include college level students.

School-based programs focusing on social influences and refusal skills have been found in significant studies to have a modest but significant effect in reducing the onset and level of tobacco use. Id at page 4. In one specific scientific study, involving the meta-analysis of smoking prevention, published between 1974 and 1991, the authors found that social influence programs could account for reductions in smoking between 5–30 percent. Id.

Our recommendations on this issue are similar to the suggestions espoused by the Centers for Disease Control and Prevention (CDC). We believe that in the State of Hawaii all public and private schools should be required to institute programs which:

a. fully explore the social influences and peer norms regarding tobacco use,

b. discuss in detail the short and long term physical and psychological consequences of smoking, and

c. completely educate school teachers on these subjects as well. Id.

5. <u>Youth Access Restrictions</u>: There is no question but that tobacco products have horrible physical, mental, and addictive effects on smokers. Unfortunately, there is also little question that tobacco products manufacturers aim their products, in large part, toward adolescents. On the same note, apparently adolescents, for a variety of reasons, are more susceptible than adults to initiating or continuing smoking.

At the very least, this legislature should take measures to insure that the widespread death and diseases caused by smoking tobacco products, is curbed in its effect against young people in this state.

Therefore, we advocate the following. We request that this legislature pass a law requiring that persons in the State of Hawaii be at least 25 years of age before they are allowed to purchase, possess, or use tobacco products. Accompanying laws should also be passed requiring the strict enforcement of this law.

6. Community Intervention: The increased understanding and awareness of environmental, social, and cultural conditions involving tobacco use has resulted in an emphasis on interventions that include comprehensive, community-based approaches. This involves the involvement of families, schools, community organizations, churches, businesses, the media, social service and health organizations, government, and law enforcement with intervention strategies generally focused on making changes in both the environment and individual behavior.

Studies involving the effectiveness of these very broad based approaches are very encouraging in many cases. Lantz, et al., page 6. School-based programs and community involvement, as listed above, have a stronger impact when they work in tandem rather than as separate, stand-alone interventions. Id at page 8. Additionally, community interventions whether they are performed separately or in tandem should be combined with increased taxation, more effective media use and policy formulation and implementation. Id.

It is extremely clear that the tobacco industry has been successful in advertising and marketing pro-tobacco messages for many decades. Mass media efforts are viewed as particularly effective for reaching youth, who are often heavily exposed to and greatly interested in media messages. Studies indicate that if the mass media messages are anti-tobacco or anti-smoking, and they are structured correctly, they would have an increased possibility of succeeding. The literature suggests that mass media interventions are much more likely to have an impact when the following conditions are met:

a. the campaign strategies are based on sound, social marketing principles;

b. the effort is large and intense enough;

c. target groups are carefully differentiated;

d. messages for particular groups are based on empirical findings regarding the needs and interests of each specific group; and

e. the campaign is of sufficient duration. Id at page 10.

We do not assume to have expertise on all the different forms of community intervention involving smoking which can be utilized to assist residents in the State of Hawaii. There are certain methods of which we are aware, however, they can be implemented by this legislature which we believe will materially decrease tobacco usage in this state. We have already discussed, at length, substantially increasing the tobacco products taxation levels. In addition, we have focused on three other tobacco use reduction efforts which we likewise suggest. For a much more effective combination though, we also want to ask this legislature to use the mass media instrumentality and make the public aware of the facts, realities and truths regarding smoking tobacco products.

7. Monitoring Performance and Evaluating Tobacco Usage Reduction Programs: Tobacco control programs today, throughout this country, build on decades of research and demonstrations. State Programs Can Reduce Tobacco Use, Institute of Medicine, National Research Council, page 9. The

scale and scope of tobacco control in the United States has grown over the last decade. Id. All of the measures suggested above can improve over time if the elements of each program is properly assessed, different strategies are evaluated and compared, and research is conducted to improve the various programs.

Legislatures need to be communicative with the public about the use of public dollars. This is not intended to imply that results will be quick; significant reductions in tobacco use may take years to accomplish. Therefore, state tobacco control measures, implemented by this Legislature, should be consistently evaluated and explicit goals formulated and coupled with performance measures.

Appendix 3

HOUSE
CONCURRENT
RESOLUTION

REQUESTING ALL MANUFACTURERS OF CIGA-
RETTES AND TOBACCO PRODUCTS TO PROVIDE
ANNUAL REPORTS TO THE DEPARTMENT OF
HEALTH ON THE CONSTITUENCY AND NICOTINE
RATINGS OF THE PRODUCTS AND REQUESTING
THE DEPARTMENT OF HEALTH TO INVESTIGATE
PUBLIC HEALTH RISKS ASSOCIATED WITH EXPO-
SURE TO THE ADDED CONSTITUENTS AND NICO-
TINE.

WHEREAS, one-third of all children who smoke regularly will
eventually die of tobacco-related causes, with 430,000 deaths
nationally and 1,400 deaths in Hawaii annually from tobacco-
related causes; and

WHEREAS, tobacco-related diseases are the leading preventable
cause of mortality and morbidity in this country for the past 50
years; and

WHEREAS, despite a massive and incredibly expensive anti-
tobacco effort through education, negative advertising, and environmental restrictions, there has been no reduction in smoking for
any societal group except for Caucasian males; and

WHEREAS, the increase in smoking is especially high for females, teenagers, native Hawaiians, and all ethnic minorities, regardless of the efforts put forth to increase knowledge and awareness of tobacco's harmful effects; and

WHEREAS, it has been publicly acknowledged that tobacco products that contain nicotine at any level are addictive; and

FDA to all states to individually examine their state laws regarding tobacco regulation; and

WHEREAS, in Hawaii the Director of Health has the authority and responsibility to control and regulate harmful consumer products, but tobacco is currently exempt from being classified as a consumer product in this state; and

WHEREAS, it is now time for Hawaii to begin regulating tobacco with the technical assistance of the FDA and other federal agencies for the safety, welfare, and economic relief of Hawaii's citizens; and

WHEREAS, the Department of Health must first gain jurisdiction by seeking the removal of tobacco as an exemption as a consumer product, then:

1. Begin the regulation process by gathering and evaluating FDA data on tobacco to study the best approach to minimize health risks; and

2. Enforce disclosure and set standards for key cigarette components;

now, therefore,

BE IT RESOLVED by the House of Representatives of the Twenty-first Legislature of the State of Hawaii, Regular Session of 2002, the Senate concurring, that this body requests all manufacturers of cigarettes, cigars, snuff, pipe tobacco, or chewing tobacco sold in Hawaii to provide annual reports to the Department of Health for the purpose of protecting public health and welfare; and

BE IT FURTHER RESOLVED that this body requests that the report should list the following for each brand of tobacco product:

1. The identity of any added constituent including tobacco and reconstituted tobacco sheet made wholly from tobacco to be listed in descending order according to weight, measure, or numerical count;

2. The nicotine yield ratings and components that affect nicotine absorption, which shall accurately reflect nicotine intake for average consumers based on standards to be established by the Department of Health;

3. The identity and quantity of toxic constituents of:

   A. Tobacco, by brand; and

   B. Cigarettes, by brand of tobacco; and

4. The identity and quantity of toxic contaminants in the mainstream and side stream smoke of cigarettes by brand and toxicity yield rating based on standards to be established by the Department of Health; and

BE IT FURTHER RESOLVED that the Department of Health, in conjunction with federal authorities, is requested to:

1. Investigate public health risks associated with exposure to added constituents, toxic ingredients, and nicotine; and

2. Develop methods and criteria for manufacturers, under regulatory guidelines, to reduce the risks associated with exposure to harmful constituents, ingredients, and nicotine; and

BE IT FURTHER RESOLVED that the Department of Health submit a report of its findings and recommendations to the Legislature no later than 20 days before the convening of the Regular Session of 2003; and

BE IT FURTHER RESOLVED that certified copies of this Concurrent Resolution be transmitted to the Director of Health and to manufacturers of cigarette and tobacco products.

OFFERED BY: _____

Report Title:
Tobacco Regulation

Appendix 4

Catholic Church Tasks Performed

I did volunteer work for many days over a period of several months at the Catholic Church in Maui, Hawaii. My daily work efforts typically lasted for about eight hours on the days I devoted to assisting this church.

Construction

The construction work I performed was in the church, rectory, school and school office. Such work was electrical, telephone, cable, plumbing, and carpentry.

Legal

Performed substantial legal research and gave advice on how to protect assets, form subsidiary corporations, and on the subject of family violence.

Appendix 5

Salvation Army Tasks Performed

I did volunteer work for hundreds of days over a period of two to three years for the Salvation Army in Maui, Hawaii. My daily work efforts typically lasted eight hours on the days I devoted to assisting this organization.

Construction

The construction work I performed was inside and outside of all four Salvation Army buildings. They included the church, the store, the meeting room and kitchen, and the Salvation Army lieutenants' home. The construction efforts I performed included almost every construction trade imaginable. The types of work efforts included installing several roofs, removing old siding and installing new siding, cutting in new doors and windows, installing new stairs and stairway ramps, performing an electrical service change and upgrade, completely renovating the entire kitchen, installing several large storage sheds outside the buildings, mounting multiple sets of shelves in all four buildings, and the list goes on and on and on.

Legal

Performed substantial legal research and gave advice on multiple issues involving the Salvation Army's existence and operations on Maui.

Appendix 6

Episcopal Church Tasks Performed

I did volunteer work for many days over a period of almost two years at the Episcopal Church in Maui, Hawaii. My typical daily work efforts varied between a few hours to a full time on the days I devoted to aiding this church.

Construction

The construction work I performed was on the church, school, and pastor's home. Such work was electrical, carpentry, plumbing, and maintenance.

Legal

Performed substantial legal research and gave advice on the church lease, church camp, and issues involving a motorcyclist group harassing the church.

Appendix 7

Methodist Church Tasks Performed

I did volunteer work for numerous days over a period of several months at the Methodist Church in Maui, Hawaii. My typical daily work efforts varied from a few hours to the entire day on the occasions I devoted to assisting this church.

Construction

The construction work I performed was in the church, church office, the school, and inside and outside of a large parking garage. Such work was painting, electrical, plumbing, carpentry, and maintenance.

Legal

I performed substantial legal research and analysis on issues regarding the standards applicable to and the operation of a preschool in Hawaii.

Appendix 8

Boys and Girls Club Tasks Performed

I did volunteer work for many days over a time period of numerous months at the Boys and Girls Club in Maui, Hawaii. My typical daily work efforts varied between a few hours to a full time on
the days I devoted to assisting this organization. All the volunteer
tasks I performed for the Boys and Girls Club was construction
work. The labor and efforts I completed was in the club area, the
offices, kitchen, bathrooms, and outside of the facilities. Such work
was carpentry, plumbing, electrical, and maintenance.

Appendix 9

Women's Outreach Program Tasks Performed

I did work for a number of days over a period of a few weeks for the Women's Outreach Program in Maui, Hawaii. My daily work efforts typically lasted a few hours on the days I devoted my time to this program. My work efforts ordinarily involved legal analysis, research, and advice for the Women's Outreach Program members. Moreover, I worked on several spousal abuse issues. Additionally, I had meetings with several officers of the program.

VOLUNTEER TASKS PERFORMED IN IDAHO

Appendix 10

Genesis World Mission Tasks Performed

I did volunteer work for many days over a period of a few months at the Genesis World Mission in Garden City, Idaho. My work efforts were usually full time on those days that I devoted to assistance of this organization. My volunteer time was spent almost exclusively on handling legal matters for Genesis World Mission. I dealt with issues involving organizational structure, limiting liability, and legal documents for use with potential clients. I also performed electrical work in the dental and medical offices of the facility.

Appendix 11

Idaho Legal Aid Office Tasks Performed

I did volunteer work for many days over a period of many months at the Idaho Legal Aid Office in Boise, Idaho. My work efforts were ordinarily full time on those days I devoted to assisting this facility. All the assistance I provided was legal. I worked on many cases and did research on a score of legal issues. I also prepared legal memorandums, analysis letters, discovery and summaries of legal developments and documents.

Appendix 12

Life Care Center Tasks Performed

I did volunteer work ordinarily three times a week for over one and a half years at the Life Care Center of Boise, Idaho. My daily work efforts there typically lasted three to five hours on the days I devoted to assisting this organization. The residents at the Life Care Center are either extremely elderly or severely disabled. They often have a myriad of medical illnesses and infirmities. Families and friends ordinarily visit them, often infrequently. Commonly, many of the Life Care Center residents have nothing to do but lie in bed and stare off into space. If they have the energy and desire, as an alternative, they may chose to watch the same television programs over and over. When I initially went to the Life Care Center, it seemed immediately obvious to me that the residents needed to be entertained in a way that would provide them with an activity which would be both meaningful and entertaining. For these reasons, I began playing various card games with many of the residents. I also initiated a public speaking club at the facility. Furthermore, I brought videotaped and DVD movies to the Life Care Center for all the residents to enjoy. Lastly, I also instituted the practice of taking a limited number of disabled residents to public movie theaters to watch recently released movies.

Appendix 13

Valley View Retirement Community Medical Wing Tasks Performed

I did volunteer work two or three days a week for over a year at the Valley View Retirement Community Medical Wing in Boise, Idaho. My daily work efforts there usually lasted two to four hours on the days I devoted to assisting this facility. Similarly to the residents at the Life Care Center, the patients on the medical wing of the Valley View Retirement Community are often very old or extremely ill. They also have a limited number of visitors and very few enjoyable and meaningful pastimes in their lives. As a result of my initial perceptions, I began several entertaining practices at that facility. I have noted that both there and at the Life Care Center I have made several strong friendships with elderly and severely disabled individuals.

978-0-595-43962-1
0-595-43962-4

www.ingramcontent.com/pod-product-compliance
Lightning Source LLC
Chambersburg PA
CBHW030320290526
45785CB00001B/440